P9-CDI-434

NOBODY'S CUTER THAN YOU

Nobody's Cuter than You

A memoir about the beauty of friendship

Melanie Shankle

Tyndale House Publishers, Inc.
Carol Stream, Illinois

Visit Tyndale online at www.tyndale.com.

Visit the author's blog at thebigmamablog.com.

TYNDALE and Tyndale's quill logo are registered trademarks of Tyndale House Publishers, Inc.

Nobody's Cuter than You: A Memoir about the Beauty of Friendship

Copyright © 2015 by Melanie Shankle. All rights reserved.

Cover illustration copyright © Tyndale House Publishers, Inc. All rights reserved.

Author photograph taken by Leslie Lonsdale, copyright © 2013. All rights reserved.

Decorative scroll artwork copyright © Creative Market. All rights reserved.

Designed by Nicole Grimes

Edited by Stephanie Rische

Published in association with William K. Jensen Literary Agency, 119 Bampton Court, Eugene, Oregon 97404.

All Scripture quotations, unless otherwise indicated, are taken from the Holy Bible, *New International Version,*® *NIV.*® Copyright © 1973, 1978, 1984, 2011 by Biblica, Inc.® Used by permission. All rights reserved worldwide.

Scripture quotations marked *The Message* are taken from *The Message* by Eugene H. Peterson, copyright © 1993, 1994, 1995, 1996, 2000, 2001, 2002. Used by permission of NavPress Publishing Group. All rights reserved.

Scripture quotations marked ESV are taken from *The Holy Bible*, English Standard Version® (ESV®), copyright © 2001 by Crossway, a publishing ministry of Good News Publishers. Used by permission. All rights reserved.

Library of Congress Cataloging-in-Publication Data

Shankle, Melanie.
    Nobody's cuter than you : a memoir about the beauty of friendship / Melanie Shankle.
        pages cm
    Includes bibliographical references.
    ISBN 978-1-4143-9748-1 (sc)
    1. Shankle, Melanie—Friends and associates.   2. Female friendship.   3. Female friendship—Religious aspects—Christianity.   I. Title.
    BJ1533.F8S465 2015
    241'.6762—dc23   2014048500

Printed in the United States of America

21   20   19   18   17   16   15
11   10   9   8   7   6   5

Author's Note

I WILL NOT even pretend like I've remembered all the events in this book exactly as they occurred. Many years have passed since some of the events happened, and—true story—I forgot to pick up my daughter's friend for a soccer game yesterday. It's safe to say that total recall of forty-plus years of life is probably not my gift. However, I have done my best to piece together memories and conversations to the best of my ability, although some names and places have been changed to protect people who may not necessarily want part of their life story told in my little book. But I have stayed true to the story of all that my friends have meant to me and how they have all been a gift in my life. I'm thankful for every bit of it, even the tough parts.

To all the friends I've had over
the course of my life:
You've made life richer, better, and
brighter than I ever dreamed.
To Tiff, who showed me what it
means to follow your heart.
To Jen, who has always been like the
North Star, pointing the way.
And most of all, to Gulley.
"If you live to be a hundred, I want to
live to be a hundred minus one day so
I never have to live without you."

A. A. Milne

Contents

Introduction

A friend is one that knows you as you are, understands where you have been, accepts what you have become, and still, gently allows you to grow.

AUTHOR UNKNOWN

I HAVE TO be honest and confess that I'd planned to write a completely different book than this one. I'd even signed a contract for it and everything. But then, because I am daring and madcap and fly by the seat of my pants, I totally changed direction and decided to write a book about friendship instead.

It also may have helped that I visited my publisher a few weeks ago, and in the middle of our meeting they said, "Hey, why don't you write a book about friendship?" And I said, "Okay."

Of course, this could have been because I'd just suggested that perhaps I should write a book called *Barley and Me: The Story of a Dog That Fought in World War II, Died, Went to Heaven, and Came Back to Tell about It*. I chose that title based on extensive research I did at my local bookstore, where I realized that the majority of bestselling books are about three things:

someone's dog
a person who fought in World War II
someone who has gone to heaven and come back to life

I guess in all fairness I could have a chance at similar success if I wrote a fiction book for teenage girls about vampires or various factions in a dystopian society or tributes being forced to fight to the death in an arena, but I am not that creative and really don't have the time because I'm too busy trying to figure out how to braid my hair like Katniss Everdeen. Here's what I've learned from that: you can pin all the pins on Pinterest, but that doesn't mean that hairstyle is actually going to happen.

Ultimately, a book about friendship seemed to make the most sense. Even when I was writing *The Antelope in the Living Room* (a memoir about marriage), my husband, Perry, told someone, "What she needs to write next is a book called *Gulley and Mel: The Real Love Story*."

A few months ago, my daughter, Caroline, curled up next to me on the couch after a day of school that had left her tired and frustrated. She began to tell me about some of the girl drama going on in the fifth grade and that she just wasn't sure who she could trust and who her real friends were. We talked through it, and I wiped her tears as she let out a big sigh, saying, "I just haven't met my Gulley yet."

And it made me want to cry because one of the things I want most for Caroline to know is the beauty of female friendship and what it adds to our lives. We need those people who will listen to our stories and hold our hands as we go through heartbreak and joy and try to figure out all that life throws our way. Those loyal soldiers who will defend us and stand with us when times get hard

and it feels like the world is against us. The women we can sur-
round ourselves with, knowing without a doubt that our names
and our hearts are safe on their tongues and in their hands.

So yes, this book is about my friendship with my best friend,
Gulley, and how we've managed to sustain our friendship over the
last twenty-five years. But it's more than that. It's about all the
friendships we as women develop over a lifetime and the influence
they have over who we were, who we are, and who we will become.
It's about the friends who wounded us and the ones who taught
us to love better.

Here's the thing: it seems that over the last couple of decades
we've substituted the joy of real friendship with cheap imitations.
We settle for "community" on Facebook and Twitter and through
a series of text messages that allow us to communicate with someone without the commitment. We have a tendency to swim in the
shallow pool of relationships because we know that getting deep
can equate to being vulnerable. And more often than not, that's a
risk we're not willing to take. It's so much easier to just text a few
happy-face emojis.

I feel like many years ago, women had a better grasp of real
friendship than we do today. Both my grandmothers had a close
circle of girl friends they called first thing every morning and
played bridge with over coffee as they shared secrets and recipes
and tips for getting the ring around the collar out of their husbands' dress shirts. (Perhaps I am basing this entire assumption on
what I used to see in those commercials for Wisk detergent.) They
rocked babies and yelled at one another's kids and diagnosed ill-
nesses. But then society changed as our world became more global
and high tech, and the simple joy of day-to-day friendship began
to fade because everyone is just so busy.

So instead, we "like" one another's beautifully filtered photos on Instagram and delude ourselves into believing we have community. But here's my question: Do we really? Do you have those people who will show up on your doorstep with food and Kleenex when the hard times come? Is there someone in your life who can look into your eyes and ask if you're okay when she already knows you're not?

Real friendship requires effort. It's showing up and laughing loud and crying hard. It's forgiving and loving and giving the benefit of the doubt. It's making a casserole, doing a last-minute car pool pickup, and making sure she knows that those cute shoes are now 50 percent off.

And that's what this book is: a memoir about the beauty of friendship. I hope it serves as a reminder to all of us that there is nothing as precious in life as a friend who knows you and loves you in spite of yourself. Because we all need those people in our lives. They serve as a mirror that allows us to see a better version of ourselves. And on those days when our jeans feel too tight and our chins have decided to embrace hormone-related acne reminiscent of our teen years and our kids have tested the limits of our sanity, a best friend will look at us and say what Gulley and I say to each other when we're having a bad day: "Nobody's cuter than you!"

And we may know that it certainly isn't the truth at that particular moment, but we'll love her for it anyway.

CHAPTER 1

Diamonds Sometimes Really Are a Girl's Best Friend

"We'll be Friends Forever, won't we, Pooh?" asked Piglet.
"Even longer," Pooh answered.

A. A. MILNE

I DROPPED OFF my daughter, Caroline, at camp for the first time ever yesterday and am in the midst of what can only be described as an emotional hangover. Perry and I helped her get her room for the week all set up, and then I hugged her good-bye as her little eyes filled with tears. At that point I basically had to sprint down the hallway without daring to cast a look back over my shoulder lest I be like Lot's wife and dissolve into a pillar of salt. Or maybe just tears.

Whatever.

Sometimes a mama likes to incorporate some Old Testament–level drama.

I managed to hold it together until I got a text from her later that night, after we'd already made the three-hour drive back to San Antonio, that read, "I'm not having fun. Please come get me," followed shortly thereafter by, "The matrices here are really hard and I can't sleep." Which confused me for a moment, because she is at soccer camp, not math camp. I felt her pain, though, because I do remember thinking that matrices were really hard back in the days when I still had to attend math classes to learn things I've never used one time in real life.

But then I realized she meant *mattresses*, not *matrices*. So maybe instead of focusing so much on soccer, we should spend some time at spelling camp.

Either way, she had begged to go to camp and gave me her word that she'd stay the whole time, and this was now one of those moments when I had to practice the art of tough love. Which is so easy in theory, but so hard when your baby girl is texting you little emojis with tears rolling down their cheeks. In short, I was like Ron Burgundy and in "a glass case of emotion."

I showed the texts to Perry and began to cry. But dads are generally the bad cop in these situations, so he was unsympathetic to her plight. He looked at me and said, "You're getting all worked up. She's safe, she's secure, and it's only for four nights. She can do anything for four nights."

Technically, I know he's right, but there's always that nagging thing inside me that realizes Caroline is our only child and if we screw this up, no one will come to visit us for Christmas when we're old. We don't have a backup plan, unless you count our dogs, and everyone knows that dogs are the worst gift givers at holidays.

So I texted my best friend, Gulley, who happened to be visiting her mom in College Station, which happens to be only five minutes away from Caroline's camp dorm. My texts were a flurry of all my feelings and emotions and anxieties, and finally Gulley texted back, "Can you just call me?"

I told her I could but if I heard her voice, I knew all I'd be able to do was cry. She replied, "You can just cry."

And so I did. I called her and sobbed all my fears and worries until I had nothing left but a bad case of the hiccups and her offer to go sleep in the dorm with Caroline if it would make me feel better.

Because there are some things that your best friend just understands in a way your husband never will. When I got off the phone an hour later, I said a prayer of gratitude that Gulley has been a constant in my life every day for the last twenty-five years. How many phone calls have we had when one of us sat and listened while the other poured out every possible emotion until there was no possibility that there were any feelings left anywhere else in the world? The answer is too many to count.

It's funny how you can have almost no memory of the first time you meet a person who eventually becomes so important to you. Some relationships are so pivotal in your life that it seems like surely you must have felt a little bit of electricity run through your veins the first time you met them—some type of jolting realization that feels like an internal neon sign flashing, "YOU'VE FOUND ONE OF YOUR PEOPLE! YOU'VE FOUND ONE OF YOUR PEOPLE!" But I really don't remember the first time I met Gulley.

After I graduated from high school, I ended up at Texas A&M by the grace of God and the generosity of my high school geometry teacher, who chose to give me a passing grade in spite of the fact I still can't come up with a proof for a theorem. Or a theorem for a proof. I can't remember, but it turns out I was right back in 1989 when I said it wasn't going to be a deal breaker to go through life without this knowledge. However, I was a master in the art of charm and bribery in the form of apple fritters, and you shouldn't underestimate how far that particular skill can take you in life.

I was so ready for a new start in a new place, and that's what College Station became for me. With one exception. I had a serious boyfriend who'd ended up at Stephen F. Austin in Nacogdoches, and I wasn't ready to let go of the relationship. So instead of immersing myself in the full Aggie experience, I spent a lot of my time driving to see my boyfriend and ultimately chose to transfer to SFA for my spring semester.

Let's all reflect for a moment on how smart and levelheaded eighteen-year-old girls are in general.

I'd made some really good friends during the fall of my freshman year, thanks to my brave step of going potluck on a roommate and hitting the jackpot with a sweet girl named Elizabeth and our suitemates, Leslie and Tiffany. But the pull of the boyfriend was too strong, and I was too insecure to walk away from the relationship at that point, even though I will be the first to admit now that the end was long overdue.

Within minutes of my arrival to Stephen F. Austin that spring, I knew I'd made a terrible mistake, but I was way too stubborn to admit it at that juncture. My boyfriend and I fought all the time, and I realized more every day that I'd given up way too much for way too little.

Anyone who knows me knows how much I love Texas A&M, and I think so much of that is because I almost let it slip out of my hands. I'll never take for granted what that university did for me—in a real way, it caused me to make one of my first adult decisions. Because when it came down to it, my desire to be back in College Station ended up being stronger than my fear of walking away from my high school boyfriend. Granted, I was only eighteen, so that decision looked a lot like calling my daddy and crying, "I've made a terrible mistake! Please help me figure out how to get back to College Station!"

When I arrived back at Texas A&M in the fall of 1990 as a sophomore, it took everything in me not to kiss the ground like a world traveler who has just returned to her homeland. I was so grateful to be back and vowed to immerse myself in every possible activity and live my college experience to the fullest. I went through sorority rush, I signed up to be part of student government, I registered to take sixteen hours, and in what turned out to be the most important decision of all, I tried out for a group known as the Diamond Darlings.

The Diamond Darlings are essentially bat girls/hostesses for the Texas A&M baseball team. They are chosen through a series of applications and interviews with athletic department personnel, and now there is even a test to assess their knowledge of baseball. The test is part of the tryout process because during my first year as a Diamond Darling, one of the girls kept referring to the umpire as the catcher.

So obviously not everyone was trying out because of a pure love of the game.

And no, that girl wasn't me. I may not know about geometry, but I know my sports.

These days I usually hesitate to mention I was a Diamond Darling, because unless someone went to Texas A&M and knows what the Diamond Darlings do, there's a certain stereotype that seems to come with saying you were a bat girl. It's kind of an assumption that all we did was hang out and date the players, which was strictly forbidden and we never did unless there were extenuating circumstances, like if he was really cute.

What people might not guess is that being a Diamond Darling gave me some of the best memories of my college career. It's the reason that to this day if I hear Van Halen singing "Top of the World" on a spring day, I feel an urge to get in my car and find a baseball game to watch. It's the reason I watch the College World Series every year and cry no matter who wins.

I'm sure I could have done other things that would have looked better on a résumé, but I guarantee those activities wouldn't have been nearly as much fun, given me as many good memories, or taught me that you should never bend at the waist to pick up a baseball bat while wearing short white shorts.

Always bend at the knees.

There are some lessons that can't be learned in a classroom.

Anyway, I'm certain I met Gulley for the first time at one of the early Diamond Darling meetings, but I can't remember the specifics. However, I do vividly remember meeting Jen, who would also become a lifelong friend, because she came sweeping into that meeting in a denim wrap skirt, Cole Haan loafers, and so much self-confidence that I found her completely and totally fascinating, especially when I found out she was only a freshman. I wasn't sure if I liked her or wanted to run away from her. I can say now that I'm glad I chose not to run.

It wasn't until later that semester that I noticed Gulley, which is so funny in hindsight because now Gulley is the type of person who lights up a room when she walks in. The party begins when she comes in, but I think she was a little more reserved back then, trying to figure out who she was and how she fit into the world. Our friendship really began when the Diamond Darlings drew names out of a hat to determine our Secret Santa recipients for the month leading up to Christmas. I opened a small piece of paper that read "Amy Gulley" and had no idea I was basically unfolding a huge part of my future.

I spent the next month buying her little gifts as part of the Secret Santa exchange. I'm sad to say that some of these gifts involved using paint pens to draw baseballs on metal tins. The college me enjoyed getting her craft on. Truthfully, the college me enjoyed anything that didn't involve studying or typing a paper on a Brother word processor or basically any activity that would have helped my grade point average.

There was even a day when I was walking through Post Oak Mall (This is the mall in College Station, although calling it a mall is kind of an insult to malls everywhere. It didn't even have a Gap back in 1990. But it did have a Foley's, a department store that sadly doesn't even exist anymore.) and discovered Gulley working at the Ski and Sea Shop. I went in to visit with her for a minute and was drawn to this sweet girl with huge brown eyes, a smile that went on for days, and an easy laugh.

Which is why I was so thankful when we ended up sitting right next to each other at the Diamond Darlings Christmas formal a few days later. Back in the early '90s, I was a girl who typically got excited about the prospect of an occasion that required a dress made by Gunne Sax with sleeves bigger than your head, but I had been dreading the Christmas formal. The boy I was dating at the time had a job that wouldn't allow him the time off to be my date, and I had no interest in going without him, especially because I didn't know the girls very well at that point and it felt pretty intimidating. Not to mention that the formal was being held at a hotel in Waco for reasons that are still not clear to me. Do you know what not one person in history has ever said without irony? "Let's go to Waco to PARTY!"

But I had been informed by the captain of the Diamond

Darlings (which is a real thing, by the way) that attendance at the formal was mandatory. So the guy I was dating arranged for his best friend to be my date, and since he lived in Waco at the time, it was easy enough for him to drive over and be my plus-one for the evening. I'm not sure why I agreed to this plan.

That's how I found myself having a truly miserable, awkward evening in Waco, Texas, with the exception of my awesome side ponytail and bangs that were teased to epic proportions. But then Gulley sat next to me because we were told to sit next to our Secret Santas, and we began to laugh and talk and, best of all, lament about our respective dates. She was there with a serious boyfriend who, unbeknownst to him, was on his way out of her life, and I was there with a boy I had virtually nothing in common with other than his best friend. Gulley and I spent that night bonding over whose date was worse, and I promise you that I won because my date was wearing a Christmas-themed sweater vest, and that's the nicest thing I can say.

As the famous line from *Casablanca* goes, "I think this is the beginning of a beautiful friendship."

Of course there was no way my mind could have comprehended all that this friendship would become. There are probably only a handful of times in our lives when someone who will change us forever walks in—when we find someone we can love with our whole hearts, who will challenge us and shape us and make us feel like the world is safer and brighter just because they are in it. A person who loves us for exactly who we are, yet teaches us to be better because of who they are and how they live their life.

A person who, twenty-five years later, will listen to you cry on the night you drop off your daughter at soccer camp.

That's Gulley.

It just took me the first nineteen years of my life to find her.

CHAPTER 2

When We Were Young

Growing apart doesn't change the fact that for a long time we grew
side by side; our roots will always be tangled. I'm glad for that.

ALLY CONDIE

SOME PEOPLE MIGHT not think it's feasible to make an entire business out of selling the leftover foil from Hershey's Kisses, but back in the summer of 1976, Lindsay Letterman and I would have told you that you were wrong. We had a vision for a potentially lucrative enterprise that involved smoothing out the foils after we ate the chocolate inside and selling them for five cents apiece. We even had a little stand set up on the neighborhood sidewalk in front of her house.

In what is probably a sad statement about American children in the 1970s, we had several paying customers. In fact, I hate to brag, but we earned upwards of thirty-five cents in two days. It probably helped that this was before the economy totally tanked in the later years of that decade, and people were still spending money freely.

And by people, I mean naive, impressionable kindergartners who found loose change on the kitchen counters of their homes.

But more important, we had a goal. We were united in our desire to make a little extra cash in the summer of '76 because we knew that at some point in the week, the ice-cream truck would turn down our street and our hard work would pay off in the form of a Dream Bar. Or, if we were really feeling fancy, one of those popsicles shaped like a foot with a gumball in place of the big toenail.

(Please excuse me. I think I just threw up in my mouth.)

I don't remember many other details about Lindsay, other than the fact that we had an ongoing argument about who was most like the Bionic Woman. She insisted that she was because her name was Lindsay, just like Lindsay Wagner, who played the Bionic Woman on TV, but I felt that this was a baseless argument. Clearly I was much more like the Bionic Woman, as evidenced by the fact that I was the one who already knew how to ride a two-wheel bicycle without training wheels.

But in spite of this huge disagreement and a business venture that ultimately failed, Lindsay Letterman is the very first friend I remember—the first person in my life whom I chose to spend time with. We ran back and forth across the street to play Barbies, and we dressed alike on Go Texan Day in kindergarten. And let me assure you, there was basically no greater display of friendship at age five than that. Even though we were most likely dressed alike because our moms found the same prairie dresses on sale at Weiner's.

But in April of my kindergarten year, we moved to a new neighborhood on the other side of Houston, and I lost touch with Lindsay in the way you do with friends you make early in life. That's because at that age friends are really more like real estate, and the most important component is location, location, location. If you're not a bike ride away, then it's time to bid thee farewell.

My family's move took us to a new neighborhood in the suburbs of Houston, because that's what everyone was doing in the mid-1970s—leaving the mean streets of the city for the greener pastures of the suburbs, where two-story brick houses and neighborhood swimming pools reigned supreme. We moved into a subdivision called Westador, which was off FM 1960. And not Old Westador, but New Westador, because the newer, the better. I remember my mom telling me that FM stood for Farm to Market Road, and it meant that this paved four-lane road used to be nothing but a dirt path that farmers used to carry their produce to the local market. It fascinated me to no end to think—in my mind, at least—that mere months before we'd moved there, the road had been covered with old men in overalls pushing wheelbarrows full of produce. In other words, I was a sucker for a Pinterest-worthy story long before Pinterest was a gleam in overachievers' eyes.

There was still a month left in the school year when we moved, and I was enrolled in a new kindergarten class just in time to participate in their theatrical performance of *The Tortoise and the Hare*. Since I was a latecomer, I was given the star-making role of Rabbit #4, and my costume consisted of a pink leotard and tights with a bonnet-like thing that had white bunny ears. It wasn't nearly as splashy as the costume a girl named Amy got to wear, which was a hot pink bunny costume complete with a yellow fur tummy. Oh, I was envious. And in fact, when Amy and I became friends and I spent the night at her house months later, I saw the bunny costume hanging in her closet and suggested that I try it on. It was rabbit perfection, just as I had imagined.

Anyway, I vaguely remember the day we moved into our new

house on Misty Lea Lane. A few things stood out to me immediately. The first was that we had a fire hydrant in our front yard. I thought that was just about the greatest thing ever, and if, at the age of five, I had been allowed to write the MLS listing of our new home, it would have read: 4 BR, 2 1/2 BA, NEW CARPET AND FIRE HYDRANT IN FRONT YARD. The other feature that took my breath away was that the house was two stories. The stairs offered endless possibilities for entertainment. And lastly, the wallpaper in the entryway was a flocked, velvety texture in a lovely shade of avocado green. I remember feeling that wallpaper with my fingertips, and if I'd known about Scarlett O'Hara back then, I surely would have been thinking, *Lawdy, we sho' is rich now.*

One of the best features of the house was that the downstairs level made a complete circle. If my friends and I wanted to play hide-and-seek, we could start in the formal living room, which led to the family room, which led to the breakfast area and kitchen and then to the dining room and back to the living room. It allowed for endless games of chase. There was also a closet in the den right next to the wet bar (a bar was a requirement in all homes in the '70s because it conveyed class and sophistication and a place to hang your Lone Star Beer mirrored tray). The closet was tucked under the stairs, and the fact that the ceiling was slanted fascinated me to no end.

All the bedrooms were upstairs, with my parents' bedroom on one side of the staircase and the other three bedrooms on the other side. I remember lying in bed at night trying to gather up my courage to walk to their room, knowing I would have to walk past the stairs. Heaven only knows what could have been lurking at the bottom of those stairs just waiting for a kid in a Holly Hobbie nightgown to walk by.

I had my own room with a brass bed and an old-fashioned bedspread with yellow flowers on it, but in reality my sister and I shared her bedroom. She had two twin beds with pink headboards, and I slept in her room every night because I gave new meaning to the word scaredy-cat. I'm not sure what kind of defense I thought a three-year-old in Winnie the Pooh pajamas would offer me from an erupting volcano or a king cobra attack (the fact that these were my two greatest fears at the time suggests that I was unaware of the geographical factors that made both scenarios highly unlikely), but I felt better knowing she was there. Plus, when insomnia hit, we had a companion right in the next bed. And my sister always kept a stash of Sun-Maid Raisins in her nightstand drawer, which in retrospect was sheer brilliance on her part.

The remaining bedroom was a guest bedroom/playroom. It was filled with our Barbies and their luxurious townhome complete with an elevator and a plastic pink couch, various baby dolls and doll beds, and a record player that enabled us to listen to the Bee Gees and Olivia Newton-John. We spent hours playing in that room, and Barbie put on several concerts outside her Winnebago with her Olivia Newton-John lip-synching skills.

One of the best things that ever happened to that house was when my parents got it professionally landscaped. The landscapers filled the yard with flower beds covered in dark pine mulch, and each flower bed had a little ditch feature around it to keep the grass from encroaching on the bed. My friends and I would fill up those little moats with water, drag Barbie out there in her Corvette, and have a good, old-fashioned Barbie campout complete with a river. It was treacherous terrain for Barbie and Ken, roughing it out there among the azaleas.

In the backyard, we had a metal swing set with pastel-colored stripes winding around the legs. This was before the metal swing set was killed off by the wooden playscape—probably because of all the tetanus shots that kids of the '70s had to get after being cut by sharp pieces of metal sticking out of seesaws.

My friends and I would spend hours swinging and jumping out of our swings. We'd twist them around and around until the chains creaked and couldn't go any tighter, and then we'd spin wildly out of control, stumbling off the swing and falling facedown in the St. Augustine grass.

The backyard also had a cement patio, and it was the scene of much of my early roller-skating choreography. I would put on my new white roller skates, which had lime-green wheels and stoppers, and come up with routines that would make the entire cast of *Xanadu* weep with envy. It was just a matter of time before a talent scout discovered me on the back patio and begged me to come to Hollywood or probably just the local Magic Skate.

Our house was on a cul-de-sac, and there was never a shortage of kids to play with, night or day. This was back in the days when parents didn't live in as much fear as we do now, and we kids were allowed to freely roam the streets of the neighborhood in pre-adolescent gangs, searching for the next game of kickball, freeze tag, or hide-and-seek. Finally, when dusk fell, mothers all up and down the street would call for their kids to come inside and eat supper. I can only imagine how much grass we killed throughout our neighborhood as we ran from yard to yard all day long.

But let's back up for a minute to the fire hydrant in my front yard, because it played a key role in my introduction to the neighborhood kids. As the movers unloaded all the boxes and furniture into our new home, I sat on that fire hydrant like it was a small metal pony, and the kids began to gather around. The first girls I met were sisters who lived two doors down. Their names were Catherine and Elizabeth Johnson, although I was informed immediately that the older one, Elizabeth, was called "Libba" by everyone and that she could dance and sing just like Olivia Newton-John. What had just happened? Had we moved to the suburbs or heaven?

I think I was already playing at their house by that afternoon, thanks to the social freedom that belongs only to kids. We lose that quality as we get older. We become more guarded and conscious of potential rejection. We usually need to meet people over coffee and make a lot of polite small talk before we're ready to invite them into our homes. But when you're young, it's just a matter of, "What? You've seen *Grease* eight times at the movie theater too? You're my new best friend! Please come to my house and spend the night."

Catherine Johnson quickly became my new best friend. She was the person I wanted to be more than anyone else in the whole world. Anyone who could flip her head over and come back up with wings that would make Farrah Fawcett weep was someone to admire.

Our moms bought us matching red satin jackets from Weiner's, and we became our own version of the Pink Ladies. I spent as many nights as possible at her house. We'd climb into her bunk beds (You don't even want to know the level of envy I had over those bunk beds. They were just like Willis and Arnold's beds on *Diff'rent Strokes*.) and whisper secrets and tell ghost stories. We rearranged the books in her closet to create a library where other neighborhood kids could check out books. We created dance routines to the entire sound track of *Saturday Night Fever* and rode our bikes all over the neighborhood in search of adventure.

Catherine introduced me to the culinary wonder that is Nacho Cheese Doritos covered in melted Cheez Whiz and another delight that consisted of sliced ham, cheese, and carrots covered in Italian dressing, which she called her "specialty." Everything with her was more exotic, more fun. She just had an air about her that seemed a little out of my league, and I felt inordinately lucky to be her friend.

To this day, I'm still not sure if her parents were married or divorced. Her dad was constantly in and out of their lives. He'd disappear for months and then show up with a new puppy or a pool table or, best of all, a jukebox. In the economy of childhood, I believed this made her the most fortunate person EVER to have a dad who brought her all those treasures. In my mind, her house was practically Disney World, but with swinging doors that separated the family room from the foyer to allow for very dramatic entrances and exits.

What I discovered many years later was that Catherine's dad was abusive. He hit his wife and sometimes even the girls. He'd show up drunk and angry, leave his mark on them, and then take off for days, weeks, or even months at a time. Then he'd return home offering extravagant gifts in exchange for forgiveness. I'm not sure how much the neighbors knew, and I guess it was a different time, when people tended to stay silent about those kinds of things.

My parents never told me any details during those years, but I remember that whenever Mr. Johnson returned home, my days of being allowed to play at Catherine's house were few and far between. I didn't understand, and it made me so mad that I couldn't go over there. After all, her house had a tire swing, not to mention a jukebox that we would use to listen to "Louisiana Saturday Night" over and over again while we played pool like two young hustlers in Jordache jeans.

At one point, Catherine's mom announced that she was taking her girls and moving away for a little while. I was devastated to lose my best friend, and I tried to fill the gap with a few other girls who lived on our street. We even formed a club that required all of us to wear the same outfit to school every Wednesday (green corduroy bell-bottoms with a Donny and Marie Osmond T-shirt, obviously), but it wasn't the same. I didn't feel the closeness with them that I did with Catherine (clearly there's something in us that knows a kindred spirit at an early age), and I really wasn't even that sad when they eventually kicked me out of the club for wearing the wrong outfit to school. In my defense, my green cords were dirty.

But then, a few months later, Catherine and her family moved back into their house, and order was restored to my world. We resumed our sleepovers and even played a new video game called Pong on the console TV in her playroom. Pong was maybe the most amazing thing I'd seen up to that point. A game you could play on your TV!

Only weeks later, I had plans to spend the night at Catherine's house when my parents informed me that we needed to have a family talk before I went over there. As they sat my sister and me down on the couch, they began to explain that they had made a decision to separate. My dad was moving into an apartment not far away the following week, and they reassured us with all the things I'm sure they'd read in a book that you're supposed to tell your kids to ease the pain that life as they know it is ending: "It's not your fault." "We'll always love you." "Sometimes mommies and daddies just can't live together anymore, but it will be fun to have a new place to visit!"

My sister was only four at the time, so I'm not even sure she understood what was going on, but at eight years old, I was old enough to know that this wasn't something I wanted to happen. Hot tears rolled down my face, and my mom suggested that maybe I should spend the night at home instead of going to Catherine's, but I insisted that I wanted to go anyway. I didn't know many details, and it would be years before I ever fully processed that moment, but I knew without a doubt that I wanted to be with my best friend that night, curled up in her bunk bed and giggling about anything other than what was really happening in my life.

We were eight years old. It wasn't like we were going to break down the psychological impact of divorce on children and all that is wrong with the American family. But I needed an escape from my reality, and that's what Catherine was for me during that time. She was my safe place where I could still be a kid and see who could make the longest black skid down the street by slamming on the brakes on our bikes or fly down the street in her go-kart, because yes, Catherine had a go-kart. I can't even pretend like my jealousy over this was in check.

But one night everything finally boiled over in Catherine's home. I learned later that her dad had shown up in a rage. He left and they fled. The house went on the market, and eventually some new neighbors moved in.

Catherine and I stayed in touch for a year or so after that. At the time, I didn't know what had happened—I just knew that her mama had decided to move them back to Arkansas, closer to the small town where she'd grown up. They came back for a visit about a year later, and when I went to see her in the Hilton Hotel where they were staying, we had so much fun catching up as we ran up and down the hallways and swam in the pool. It was like old times watching her flip that perfect hair and ooze coolness that I could only dream about. If I could have chosen between being like Catherine or being like Jo Polniaczek from *The Facts of Life*, I would have picked Catherine, and that is really the highest compliment I had in my arsenal at that juncture in life.

But eventually we quit writing letters, and this was back in the olden days when it wasn't a cheap proposition to call someone long-distance, especially when all you were going to talk about was *Urban Cowboy* and how much you loved John Travolta. Not to mention that, looking back, I realize Catherine and her family were probably always on the run from her dad and never stayed in one place for very long.

Now that I know more about her childhood (and I'm sure there is even more that I don't know), it makes me sad to think about what was going on inside this poor little girl and even more sad to realize that I thought she had it all because she was allowed to wear her mom's Candie's shoes.

In those young years of friendship, you know so much about your best friend—her favorite color, which TV show she likes best, the blue shorts she likes to wear, and what song she always requests at the skating rink. But there are so many deeper things you don't know because you're just kids, and you don't know how to articulate what makes you hurt or feel scared. There is no easy way to say, "My life isn't what it seems," because it's the only thing you know, and you're not even sure it's not normal.

When I think of those years of my childhood, I recall the

yellow, two-story house on Misty Lea Lane with the white shut-
ters and the mailbox out front that my grandfather Big Bob built,
which was a perfect replica of the actual house. This was the place
where I built some of my earliest memories: long summer nights
filled with fireflies and kick the can, Fourth of July block parties
in the cul-de-sac, walks home from the bus stop after a long day
of school, and rides up and down the block on my blue bike with
the flowered banana seat while Catherine rode her Green Machine
right next to me.

But more than that, it was the place where I first learned the
joy of having a best girl friend who knows how to make you laugh
and shares her favorite books and lets you sleep on the top bunk.
It was in those years when I got my first glimpse of what it means
to have a confidante and a conspirator, and the emptiness you feel
when that person leaves your life.

CHAPTER 3

Happy Campers

We'll keep you close as always / It won't even seem you've gone / 'Cause our hearts in big and small ways / Will keep the love that keeps us strong.

MICHAEL W. SMITH

I SPENT A lot of my fourth-grade school year making up elaborate story lines that I acted out using the pickle slices that came on top of the hamburgers served in the cafeteria at Bammel Elementary School. I realize this bit of information probably just destroyed any credibility I previously had with you. Which is why I'd be better off not telling you that I also did the same thing with acorns during recess.

In my defense, it was a perfect way to pass the time at recess, because as much as I might have preferred to play on the new wooden playscape complete with a metal fireman pole, I just couldn't handle the crowd of kids that pushed and shoved their way onto it every day. (This is the same personality trait that doesn't allow me to attend any type of festival, no matter how tempted I may be when I hear that they're offering grilled meat on a stick.) And so I resorted to playing with acorns and the occasional contraband pickle I smuggled out of the cafeteria.

The good news is that I wasn't alone in my love of an activity that most likely serves as a harbinger of social isolation. My best school friend, Jill Lindsey, encouraged and participated in both "Pickle People" and "Acorn People," as we so cleverly coined this pastime.

I first met Jill in second grade, but our friendship turned into full-blown devotion when we ended up in the same homeroom for fourth grade. We were two like-minded souls who had found each other, as evidenced by our shared love of memorizing various TV commercials and singing the jingles over and over again like they were Top 40 hits. There was a time when our poor teacher grew weary of hearing us hum the Diet Pepsi commercial again and again and thought she could shame us out of our deviant behavior by making us stand up and sing it in front of the class.

What she didn't know was this was precisely the opportunity Jill and I had been waiting for. We were like Barbra Streisand in *A Star Is Born* as we proudly stood in front of our class in our Gloria Vanderbilt jeans and belted out, "Now you see it; now you don't! Here you have it; here you won't! Oh, Diet Pepsi, one small calorie. Now you see it; now you don't!"

(I need you to know I just wrote that entire thing from memory. Which is both simultaneously encouraging and disheartening, considering I forgot to pack a sandwich in my daughter's lunch box yesterday.)

(Dear Caroline, sorry you were hungry yesterday, but your mom will always be here for all your 1980s commercial-jingle needs.)

Throughout that school year, Jill and I lived through everything from the attempt on President Reagan's life to the day we tied our shoelaces together in an ill-advised attempt to be able to go home from school together, only to be informed by Mrs. Burke that we couldn't leave her classroom until we'd untied all the double knots we'd tied with great enthusiasm.

But I did go home with Jill many days after school, and it was through those playdates that I met Jenna and Jodi. They both lived around the corner from Jill, and the four of us quickly became a tight-knit little group. I obviously experienced some sadness that my name didn't start with a *J* like theirs did, because this kept us from naming ourselves "the four *J*s." But they began referring to me as Melvin in an ode to Mel Sharples from the TV show *Alice*, and I found solace in this as only a fourth grader who plays with pickles and acorns can.

The four of us became close friends, and we begged our parents to send us to Camp Cullen for a week together that summer. They did—probably because they were deathly tired of listening to us sing the McDonald's commercial from the back of the station wagon as they drove us home from Brownies meetings.

We packed up our footlockers and went to camp together. In all honesty, I don't remember many details from that week, except that we had to walk outside our cabin to go to the bathroom at night, and I nearly tipped over a canoe. But there is one huge, life-altering thing that happened. Our counselor, Carla, who was probably all of seventeen, even though I thought she was very worldly and sophisticated, introduced me to the music of Amy Grant.

Let's not even pretend that this was anything other than a pivotal moment.

As the week went on, we listened to Amy Grant sing "Mountain Top" approximately 1,754 times. It had been a hard year for me in so many ways. My parents had divorced, my mom had remarried, and in spite of all the fun I'd had with my friends, there were some moments when I'd found myself in the school counselor's office to "process" my anger and sadness. I don't remember much about these sessions except that the counselor always wanted me to draw pictures depicting how I felt. Because, sure, a bunch of stick figures can totally sum up the complex emotions of a nine-year-old girl.

But listening to the lyrics of Amy Grant's songs began to bring peace to something inside me. I'd accepted Jesus into my heart during Sunday school at some point in my early elementary school years, but this was the beginning of a deeper relationship.

And I was able to share that experience with Jill, Jodi, and Jenna. We certainly didn't have deep theological discussions, but we sang about Jesus together, which marked the first time that faith and friends coincided in my life. That summer at camp was a turning point in both my faith in Christ and the way I viewed my friends.

The four of us remained inseparable during fifth grade, and the following summer we decided it would be fun to have a week of "camp" in Jill's backyard instead of actually going to Camp Cullen. In what can only be described as wild optimism, her parents agreed to this idea, and we began to make extensive plans to spend a week in the new greenhouse Jill's parents had built in their backyard. We dubbed it "Camp Lindsey," and I'm only sad to say we didn't have T-shirts printed.

Jill's mom drove us to vacation Bible school at a nearby church every morning, and we'd spend our afternoons swimming at the neighborhood pool until it was time to come home and curl up in our sleeping bags on the floor of the greenhouse. At one point we got in one of those arguments that tend to occur among ten-year-olds, which led Jenna to climb the fence to go home, followed by Jodi, who took off down the street to her house. Jill and I chased them both down, and I guess we all engaged in some serious conflict resolution, because we managed to make it through the rest of the week. We spent the rest of that summer riding our bikes to one another's houses, to the pool, and to the nearby Stop-N-Go to buy all manner of candy and ICEEs. We listened to Hall & Oates, prank-called boys, and played Jill's new Atari.

As we ventured into the new waters of middle school the following year, the four of us began to drift apart a bit. We met new friends and more often than not found ourselves in separate classes. What I remember most about sixth grade is that, for the first time, I began to feel insecure. I was hesitant where I'd been bold and fearful where I'd been brave, and I think I began to falter in my friendships as I worried more about what people thought of me.

At the end of that school year, my mom announced we were moving to Beaumont. Her parents lived there, and her second marriage had just ended, and we all needed a change. Plus, it seemed like a fun adventure to think about starting all over again and living just down the street from Nanny and Big Bob.

We sold the house and moved over the summer, but I stayed in touch with Jodi, Jill, and Jenna for a while. As much as I craved the new, I still embraced the old and familiar. We went back to Camp Cullen together the summer between seventh and eighth grade, and one week their parents bravely put them on a Greyhound bus to Beaumont to spend time at my grandparents' lake house.

As time went on and each of us became immersed in our

separate worlds, I lost touch with Jodi and Jenna. Jill and I still saw each other on occasion throughout high school until we went off to different colleges. But I still thought about her from time to time and wondered where she was and what had happened to her.

Many years later, along came a nifty little invention called Facebook. I'd occasionally search for Jill to see if I could find her, but I never had any success. Then one day, an unmistakable picture of her popped up when I searched her name. It took me all of two seconds to send her a message in an attempt to reconnect. She immediately messaged me back, and we went back and forth sharing memories and laughing about "Pickle People" and Camp Lindsey and the fun we'd had all those years ago.

In one of those strange coincidences that sometimes happen, Jill was actually about to move to San Antonio with her husband and baby boy. We made plans to meet at my house, and the morning before she came over, I was nervous and wondered if we'd have anything to talk about. I live in fear of awkward moments and silences where words are supposed to be.

But she wasn't even in my house five minutes before it was like no time had passed at all. We laughed and filled each other in on the last twenty years of our lives. I kept looking at her in amazement, seeing both the woman she'd become and the little girl I'd known all those years ago. The sparkle in her brown eyes and the way she tells a story—all so familiar even after so much time.

And it made me realize that we often find our people at an early age. The ones who encourage us, love us, and share our weird desire to play with sliced dill pickles in the cafeteria and sing commercial jingles. The years may change our faces, our bodies, and our lives, but there are connections we make early on that remain part of who we are forever.

CHAPTER 4

The First Cut Is the Deepest

*Someday you're gonna look back on this moment of your life as
such a sweet time of grieving. You'll see that you were in mourning
and your heart was broken, but your life was changing.*

ELIZABETH GILBERT

A FEW MONTHS AGO, my best friend, Gulley, finally watched *Frozen*.
She has two boys, so her family hadn't gotten swept up in the "Let
It Go" madness like the rest of the world, and she didn't yet under-
stand why I was occasionally compelled to break out in a round of

> *Let it go, let it go!*
> *Can't hold it back anymore.*
>
> *Let it go, let it go!*
> *Turn away and slam the door.*

(I mean, seriously, that song is like crack for women of all ages.)
I'd told Gulley repeatedly that she needed to watch it—that

it was perhaps my favorite of all the Disney movies. Olaf was hysterical, Anna and Elsa were perfect, and of course the music was gorgeous. Given my feelings about it, I was surprised when Gulley called me immediately after she watched it and declared, "Well, that was the worst movie ever. The first ten minutes nearly put me in the bed."

I asked why, and she replied, "That whole 'Do You Want to Build a Snowman?' scene is the worst! Elsa just shuts Anna out and doesn't tell her why. You know that's my worst nightmare—that someone will just cut me out with no warning and I won't ever know what I did wrong. It was gut wrenching to watch."

Which is why we have now added a vow to our friendship that we will never ever "Do You Want to Build a Snowman?" each other. That we will always talk things out and never allow miscommunication to derail our relationship.

But the whole conversation made me think about times in my life when I've felt that way, like I've been dropped with no sign that it was about to happen. And I think Gulley is right—it's the worst feeling in the world because it leaves you feeling completely helpless.

I have no doubt this has happened to all of us at one point or another—otherwise it wouldn't bring up so many emotions—but for me the time that stands out most was in junior high. Which is a time not generally known as a hallmark of kindness among peers. There's a valid reason why many people believe junior high is what you spend the rest of your life getting over.

I had walked the halls of George C. Marshall Middle School for only about a week when I saw something that caused me to reevaluate all my life goals. Granted, I didn't really have many life goals up to that point, but everything I'd once thought important paled in comparison to what I saw that day. It was one of the eighth-grade cheerleaders, and she was wearing the official uniform of the Marshall Raiders cheerleading squad.

The outfit consisted of a red cheerleading skirt paired with a gray top with puffed sleeves and, be still my heart, a red-and-gray sailor's collar tied in a jaunty knot in the front with the cheerleader's name embroidered on the back. I'd never been so totally enamored with an ensemble. Which is saying something, considering all the time I spent in the juniors department at Foley's coveting various Esprit outfits.

Other than the brief period of time in the summer after fifth grade when I wanted to become a professional roller skater (thank you, *Xanadu*!), I hadn't put much thought into my future. But the day I saw that uniform, I knew I would not rest until I became a cheerleader. Never mind that the only way I could jump higher than two inches off the ground was when I was on a trampoline or that my only gymnastics experience consisted of three months in third grade when I learned that it felt unnatural to try to propel your body through the air. I was determined to become a cheerleader because the uniform had an EMBROIDERED SAILOR COLLAR.

It was good that I had that goal to get me through my seventh-grade year, because it was tough being the new girl. After the initial fascination with me wore off, everyone went back to the same cliques they'd been a part of since elementary school. Junior high girls aren't generally known for their kind and welcoming ways, and my experience proved to be no exception to this rule. These are the years that are a bad cocktail of insecurity, hormones, and believing you know all there is to know about life while you incessantly worry about whether your boobs are ever going to show up.

It didn't help that I'd chosen Jordache baggy jeans with front pleats as the essential component of my back-to-school wardrobe, only to discover that all the girls at my new school wore Levi's 501s. They were also much more knowledgeable about the world than my friends at my old school in Houston, as evidenced by the fact that a few of them cornered me after lunch one day to ask me a couple of questions about males and females using terms and phrases I didn't even know existed. At that point in my life, the extent of my experience regarding the opposite sex involved calling boys and hanging up on them (a coming-of-age art form that has been made obsolete by caller ID and smartphones) and what I saw on *The Love Boat*.

I was struggling to find my way and spent most of that year bouncing between different groups of friends as I tried to find where I fit in. I missed the casual ease and familiarity of my friendships with Jodi, Jill, and Jenna, and I longed for the days when every Friday night meant a sleepover at a friend's house and every Saturday was spent riding bikes around the neighborhood in search of adventure.

Later that spring I did manage to acquire my first boyfriend. He was a sweet sixth grader named Timothy, and our relationship basically began at Jamie Johnson's birthday party. It was a dance party held in her garage, and I could tell you a really dramatic love story about how our eyes met across Jamie's dad's lawn mower and tool bench, but the truth is I think we were the most shy, awkward people at the party, and our friends basically forced us to dance together. It's hard to believe with that type of foundation the relationship only lasted three weeks.

(I also have to interject that as I'm writing this, my daughter, Caroline, just started junior high, and I cannot even handle the thought of her having a boyfriend. What on earth? She should still be eating mashed bananas and drinking out of a sippy cup. I'm assuming you'll support me in my decision to tell her that boyfriends are something you don't have until your midtwenties. Thank you.)

(On a related note, the other night she asked me if a woman gets pregnant every time she has sex, and when I told Perry about it later, he said, "I hope you told her YES.")

At the end of the school year came the moment I'd been waiting for since the first week of school: cheerleading tryouts. I faithfully attended the after-school clinics each day and practiced the cheer over and over until I could do it in my sleep. In fact, I learned that cheer so well that I could perform it for you right now, but you'd be surprised at how many people don't want to see a forty-three-year-old woman do a cheerleading routine.

Fortunately, this was back in the days when tryouts were in front of the whole school, and the students voted for who they wanted instead of having real judges; otherwise, I feel my lack of general cheerleading acumen and vertical jump limitations wouldn't have allowed me to make the squad. But I did make it, and I didn't even try to play it cool when they announced my name over the loudspeaker as one of the Marshall Middle School cheerleaders for the upcoming school year. If Twitter had existed back then, I would have tweeted the news with #nooneiscoolerthanme at the end. Which is just one of the many reasons why I'm glad my youth didn't include social media.

That summer was full of cheerleading camps and activities, and for the first time since we moved to Beaumont, I felt like I was part of a group. I had girl friends who would call me on the phone and invite me to sleepovers and to the movies, which was important because this was the summer *Footloose* came out, and we had to see it at least 462 times. Between making new friends and knowing I'd soon get to wear that embroidered sailor collar, I was regaining much of the security I'd lost and felt confident again for the first time since elementary school.

Eighth grade started, and I had all that a girl could possibly want: a great new Esprit outfit, a sassy bi-level haircut, an add-a-bead necklace, cheerleader status, and a group of friends. In particular, I had a best friend. Over the summer I'd grown close to another girl on the cheerleading squad named Jane. Her family had moved to town in the middle of the previous year, so we bonded as two girls who were both desperately looking for a friend. It wasn't long before we were spending every Friday night at each other's houses and talking for hours on the phone about important things like what we were going to wear to school and if we liked Prince or Michael Jackson better. We had a huge spiral notebook that we wrote notes in and passed to each other between classes. That notebook was a monument to various bubble-letter stylings, pre-teen angst, and our crushes on the boy of the week. We'd doodle the words to REO Speedwagon songs and sympathize that we, too, couldn't "fight this feeling any longer." We signed every note LYLAS! (Love ya like a sister!) with puffy hearts and smiley faces and the occasional drawing of a dog, if we felt particularly creative.

Jane's friendship gave me a feeling of belonging to someone. It made me feel loved and secure and valuable. I came out of my shell and became a girl who was brave enough to act silly in the hallways and sing a duet for the school choir performance. I went out of my way to make new friends and wanted everyone around me to feel as happy as I was. I was even voted "Most Friendly" in the yearbook superlatives, which is a supreme feat of strength for someone who has always leaned heavily on the side of introvert.

(Side note: I used to think I was shy in the days before I realized I was an introvert. Now I realize I'm not afraid to talk to new people; I'm just sometimes not in the mood.)

As our eighth-grade year drew to a close, Jane and I planned out the summer before we would enter high school. We basically wanted to sleep over at each other's houses almost every night, spend as many days as possible floating in the water at my grandparents' lake house, go to the movies, and wander aimlessly around Parkdale Mall for hours at a time in search of the perfect polo shirt. I realize this all sounds very ambitious, but we felt we were up to the task.

This was back in the days before someone decided that kids need to wear a cap and gown and walk to "Pomp and Circumstance" to commemorate every single milestone in life. (I'm not kidding. We are a breath away from this type of celebration when our kids are officially potty trained. Graduation has jumped the shark. I say this as a mother who just sat through a two-hour fifth-grade graduation ceremony that included so much hype that you'd think we were sending these kids off to join the Peace Corps.) And so the end of middle school was celebrated with a festive picnic at the park across the street from the school. They had booths set up like a carnival, everyone brought a sack lunch, and we could play games or indulge in the favored activity of most thirteen-year-old girls: walking around talking about people in an attempt to make yourself feel better about your own insecurities.

It was during this picnic when someone came over to where I was happily enjoying the last hours of eighth grade to inform me that Jane was mad at me and didn't want to be my friend anymore.

I felt like I'd just been slapped in the face. I had no idea what I'd done wrong and immediately went to find Jane so we could work it out. But a circle of girls had formed around her like drama-seeking missiles looking for a target, and she refused to talk to me. The next hour was a back-and-forth game with all the informational reliability of the old game of telephone, and the story I finally got was that someone had told Jane I'd called her a witch. (The truth is, they said I'd called her a word that *rhymes* with "witch," but I'm not going to bother to type it out here, because it will just get edited out, and I think we're all grown-ups and know which word I'm talking about.)

I was stunned. The worst part was that it was a lie. I hadn't said that about her. I never would have said that about her. I'm sure I was by no means a perfect friend who did no wrong, but I'd fallen victim to someone who had decided to tell lies about me. And the most hurtful piece of the entire puzzle was that Jane was so willing to believe it and sever the friendship over a game of who-said-what. I went home that day in tears, reeling from the events of the afternoon. The summer before me no longer seemed full of promise—it was full of heartbreak in that way your heart breaks wide open in the years before you learn to protect it a little bit more.

Over the next few weeks I kept calling Jane, and she'd answer because this was before caller ID existed, but as soon as she heard my voice, she'd hang up. She began to spend time with a new group of friends, and I was totally cut out of the equation. Seeking solace, I started hanging out with my friends from church youth group who all went to different schools and were unaware of the fact that I had become an outcast in my former group. And while I had fun with them, I still missed Jane and began to dread starting a new school year with what felt like no social identity.

This was the year that Amy Grant's album *Unguarded* came out, which I remember as being kind of controversial because it wasn't a purely Christian album. This seems laughable now when you look at where music has gone. Really? We were worried about Amy Grant singing "Love will find a way"? I mean, it's not like she was trashing the hotel room and getting drunk from the contents of the mini-bar like some musicians today.

In the midst of my broken friendship, I found so much comfort in Amy Grant's music. I turned off Cyndi Lauper, and Amy's song "The Prodigal" became the theme of my summer. I still know all the words, because I sang them on constant repeat to my bedroom mirror that summer.

> *I'll be waiting*
> *I may be young or old and gray*
> *Counting the days*
> *But I'll be waiting*

All I wanted was for Jane to be my friend again. The whole thing was such an enormous misunderstanding, and even now, from a grown-up perspective, I have no idea what happened. I just know that it was the first time I'd ever been hurt that deeply by someone I loved, and it changed me. All the confidence I'd gained was gone. I felt alone and insecure and completely unprepared to begin high school on such unsure footing.

Later in life I would have breakups with boyfriends that would make me have occasional nighttime dreams that we'd gotten back together, but that summer before ninth grade was the first time I'd ever had those dreams where you wake up thinking you'd been reunited only to remember it was just a dream. Jane was, in so many ways, my first real heartbreak. Which just goes to prove that there are so many intangible things we gain from female friendship— love, acceptance, understanding—that go beyond any romantic relationship. In the movie *Jerry Maguire*, Tom Cruise's character tells Renée Zellweger, "You complete me." But the truth is, we need our friends. I mean, we need Jesus to truly complete us, but we absolutely need our girl friends, because no man wants to listen to all the words we have to say in the course of a day.

Eventually the summer came to an end, as it always does, and it was time to start ninth grade. My high school had a separate campus for the freshmen, so I knew my only option was to find a new group from among the other kids my age. And I did. I made some new friends and grew closer to a few girls I had known for a while but had never taken the time to *really* get to know. But then I'd see Jane across the cafeteria, or she'd walk right by me in the hallway as if she didn't know who I was. She was always surrounded by friends, which just added to my misery.

The interesting thing, looking back, is that she'd fallen in with a group that was a lot faster than we had been. There was talk of drinking and parties on the weekends, and now I see that, in many ways, the sudden end of our friendship was God's hand moving in my life when I couldn't see it or understand. At that point I was in no way strong enough to stand up to peer pressure, and I have no doubt I would have gone along with what the crowd was doing. My saving grace was that this faster crowd didn't want me, which I believe was an answer to prayers I didn't even know I had.

And this certainly doesn't mean that I didn't have years of bad decisions ahead of me. My desire to belong and be part of a group would still cause me to make some ill-advised choices throughout high school and college as I wobbled perilously on that line between wanting to be a good girl while believing that maybe the bad girls were having more fun.

Just recently I was doing Beth Moore's *Children of the Day* Bible study, and in the opening session she says that Paul traveled to Thessalonica with Silas and Timothy, but that prior to this voyage Paul's constant companion had been Barnabas. Apparently Paul and Barnabas had a disagreement and decided to go their separate ways. In the study, Beth says that sometimes God brings relationships to an end as a way to move us along to where he has called us to go.

I believe that is what happened during this time in my life. God had other things for me, and he knew me so much better than I knew myself, so he moved me along to a new place. It certainly didn't lessen the pain at the time, but if I've learned anything along the way, it's that sometimes the best lessons are the ones that hurt the most. If I could go back and tell my fourteen-year-old self one thing, it would be that all things truly work together for good, and that I was going to come out of this as a better person with a new perspective I'd need during my growing up years. It was the beginning of learning that I can't look to any one person to be my security blanket, and that my value goes deeper than one person's opinion of me. I learned that friendships are fragile and we need to handle them with respect and reverence. And I learned that my friends from youth group added a different kind of value to my life because we shared our faith in Christ and encouraged each other in ways that went beyond drawing puffy hearts and bubble letters.

At the end of ninth grade, Jane and I ended up having a long talk in the school library and worked things out. I don't remember all that was said, but we both apologized for any misunderstandings, and from that time on we'd say hi in the hallways or smile at each other across the cafeteria. Still, things were never the same. We never shared any more secrets or whispered to each other on the phone late into the night. Time brought new friends and healing, even though I was left with a little piece of scar tissue on my heart, which made me a little slower to immerse myself in another person. This scar made me more cautious, and ultimately it was part of what God used to shape me into the person he wanted me to be.

CHAPTER 5

The Chapter with More than Its Share of '80s References

If we listened to our intellect we'd never have a love affair. We'd never have a friendship. We'd never go in business because we'd be cynical. Well, that's nonsense. You're going to miss life. You've got to jump off the cliff all the time and build your wings on the way down.

RAY BRADBURY

SEVERAL YEARS AGO I received an unexpected phone call from my best friend from high school. We hadn't exactly lost touch over the years. I'd gone to her wedding, and she'd planned to go to mine, but then she had her first baby the week before my wedding, which tends to throw all social plans out the window, what with all the non-sleeping and feeling like a dairy cow. We'd send each other Christmas cards every year with smiling faces and well wishes, and on occasion we'd run into each other when I was back in my hometown.

So I was surprised when my mother-in-law told me that someone named Becky had called her house looking for me. I guess this is a clear indicator of how little Becky and I really knew about each other at that point in life, given that she didn't have my telephone number. My mother-in-law is always one to err on the side of caution, which probably explains why my husband continually lectures me on all the dangers of the world, so she'd written down Becky's number to give to me instead of giving Becky my number.

I couldn't imagine why she was calling but assumed it had something to do with our twenty-year high school reunion being right around the corner. Maybe she wanted me to sign up for the decorating committee or something, because I believe our mad skills with helium balloons and crepe paper for our junior-year homecoming dance was the stuff of which legends are made.

I can't remember the first time Becky and I met, but I know when I wanted to become her friend. We were in the same biology class during our sophomore year, and I was immediately drawn in by two things: (1) her dry, sarcastic humor, which she used in a way that was charming but not mean, and (2) the fact that she had a short, classic bob haircut among a sea of girls with perms that defied all the laws of hair science.

Truth be told, I'm pretty sure the reason we hadn't had any classes together up to this point was that Becky was super smart and in all honors classes, whereas I tended to err on the side of mediocrity, as evidenced by all my report cards, which read, "Does not work to potential." This is a nice way to say, "She's kind of lazy and focused on social pursuits. And her hair." Becky had this air of confidence about her—the kind of confidence that comes from knowing you are mentally superior to most of the people around you. I was delighted by the way she was able to tease our biology teacher and get a laugh from him every day, even when he wanted to act annoyed. And as I write this, I'm remembering that when she walked into the room, he would often sing to the tune of the Commodores' song "Brick House" because her last name fit perfectly. In hindsight, that might not have been entirely appropriate, but this was the 1980s and no one thought anything of it except that it was hilarious.

Over the course of our sophomore year, Becky and I grew closer and closer. And our friendship was officially sealed when my boyfriend, who was a senior, broke up with me three weeks before his prom. There have been wars fought with less drama and angst. I already had a dress that would make Scarlett O'Hara wish for a fuller skirt, and now I had no place to wear it. I dreaded going to school because I'd have to see him in the halls, and I frequently asked to go to the nurse's office, where I'd call my mom and beg her to let me come home, but I was always told to get my behind back in class. But Becky's friendship was a constant during that time. We'd pass notes back and forth between classes, talk on the phone for hours, and meet at the mall to walk around aimlessly. She helped me get through the breakup and made me laugh, and this solidified our growing friendship.

We spent the whole summer before our junior year together, and we were beyond ecstatic when we both got our long-awaited driver's licenses on our respective August birthdays. It is truly a terrible fate to be an August baby when all your friends have already turned sixteen and you're among a pitiful few who still have to experience the horror that is your mom dropping you off at the movies.

My dad bought me a Honda CR-X for my birthday. Some of you may not be aware of the Honda CR-X because, not shockingly, they don't make them anymore. It was essentially a predecessor to the Smart cars of today, because it was about the smallest thing on the road. It was a two-seater with a hatchback, and I cannot even tell you how much I loved that car. Of course, considering that my second choice was a Suzuki Samurai, you would be wise to question my vehicular judgment.

Also, I wouldn't have been nearly as excited about my Honda CR-X had I known I would drive it until the year after I graduated from college and finally bought myself a new car. By the time I traded it in, the driver's side door could only be opened from the outside, which is super cool if you're a fifth grader watching the Duke brothers on *The Dukes of Hazzard* but supremely embarrassing if you're a twenty-two-year-old college graduate arriving at a job interview. On the plus side, my college friends always joked that if they saw it parked on campus, they knew they could just open the hatchback that no longer locked and crawl inside to take a quick nap.

Anyway, Becky also received a car that summer, but we deemed my car to be the cooler car of the two for reasons I can no longer remember quite as well as I recall the duct tape I had to use to hold one of the front headlights in place only a few years later. It was decided that I should pick Becky up for school every morning because her house was only ten minutes out of my way and there was a Texaco mini-mart between her house and the school where we could pick up powdered Donettes as part of a nutritious, balanced breakfast. I'd screech into her driveway—already running five minutes late—and she'd scramble into the front seat. We'd blare Tiffany's "I Think We're Alone Now" while, in an attempt to beat the first tardy bell, I drove over the railroad tracks so fast that my little Honda CR-X practically became airborne, like the General Lee flying across a creek bank to elude Boss Hogg. Maybe it was foreshadowing its future of having doors that no longer opened.

The only thing that saved us from receiving too many tardy slips, which would have resulted in detention, was that we had history with Coach Stout for first period. Coach Stout wasn't really concerned with promptness and also had a love for the donuts we'd bring him as a peace offering (bribe is such a dirty word) if he'd overlook our late status. Considering that history class basically consisted of filling in the blanks on a few mimeographed worksheets, I don't believe we missed anything crucial. Although, this may explain why I learned more about the Revolutionary War from watching Mel Gibson in *The Patriot* than I ever learned about it in high school.

Sadly, first-period history was one of only two classes we shared due to Becky's brilliance. She was in trigonometry as a junior and had the great fortune of being in that class with a whole group of really cute senior boys. It's the only time in my life when I've ever been sad that I'm not better at math. Who cares about being able to balance a checkbook? I needed real incentive. Cute boy incentive. The only upside was that Becky had trig right after lunch each day, so I would unselfishly walk with her from the cafeteria to the classroom, and if I just so happened to have the opportunity to flirt with one of the cute senior boys as I loitered shamelessly outside the classroom until right before the bell rang, then so be it. Also, I may have brought candy with me every day to draw them in. So maybe I wasn't gifted in math, but I was gifted in other ways. Not that it ever got me a date with one of them, but whatever.

There are so many details about that year that I can't recall (probably because my brain has chosen to store the lyrics to vintage television jingles instead), yet it was my favorite year of high school. Becky and I were giddy with our newfound driver's license freedom and spent hours just driving around listening to Debbie Gibson or Madonna and later The Cure and Erasure because we decided that maybe we were a little edgy. Part of our routine was to make what we called "the rounds." This was a fancy term for driving by the house of every guy we potentially had a crush on. Some of them knew we existed, and others probably didn't. To this day I'm not sure what we were hoping for, considering that if we ever had the slightest inkling that one of them was actually outside, we'd speed up and fly down the street in hopes that they wouldn't see us. I believe the word you're looking for is *smooth*.

(This is the first time I've ever publicly admitted to "the rounds." And even now that I'm a grown, married woman with a child, there are still people whom I hope don't read this and find out they were right in thinking that they kept seeing the same black Honda CR-X drive by their house fifteen times in the course of an afternoon.)

Sometimes you have a moment in your life when you are on top of the world, when you feel invincible—like life has peaked and couldn't possibly get any better. Thankfully that hasn't held true of my junior year in high school, but it felt that way at the time. It was during that year that the movie *Dead Poets Society* came out, and I watched it endlessly with all the conviction that I was living my version of carpe diem. Becky and I were seizing the day and sucking the marrow out of every part of our high school experience in our own little way, which happened to involve attending parties in open fields, abandoned warehouses, and anyone's house where the parents happened to be gone for the weekend and the wine coolers flowed freely, because clearly we were all very sophisticated. Both of us had the security of being loved and understood by a best friend. Someone we felt comfortable enough with to admit that sometimes we felt awkward or insecure or unsure about decisions we were making now and contemplating for the future.

It felt safe. That's the best way I know how to put it: Becky made me feel safe. Loved, understood, and safe.

But any time you attempt to put all your faith in another human being, it's inevitable that it will lead to disappointment. The first little crack in our friendship had come earlier that school year, when the boy I was dating decided he didn't really like Becky. I now realize that came from his own insecurity, but it made me feel conflicted until we ultimately broke up due in large part to my loyalty to my friend. Then in the spring of our junior year, Becky and I both decided to try out for cheerleading, which was essentially the holy grail for high school girls in the late '80s. We began taking cheerleading classes (yes, this was a thing) at a local gym and talked endlessly about how fun it would be to cheer together during our senior year.

Here's something you need to know about me that I can safely admit now. I am not, nor have I ever been, cut out to be a cheerleader. The only time in my life I have ever executed a beautiful toe touch was on a trampoline. I have no ups, and my coordination is questionable at best. All the cheerleading lessons in the world weren't going to change that. My only hope would have been Mary Lou Retton inhabiting my body on the day of tryouts, and, well, that kind of stuff only happens in horror movies. So it should have come as no surprise that Becky made it as a varsity cheerleader and I did not. I wanted to be happy for her. I did. I wanted to so badly. But the problem is that when you're an insecure sixteen-year-old who hasn't even learned to love herself or to find her value in things that matter, it's hard, if not impossible, to love someone else unselfishly.

I went out for a celebratory dinner that night with Becky and her family, but I was devastated. All I could think was that I was the one who'd decided to try out in the first place, and she tried out just because I was doing it, and it wasn't fair, and now she was going to be best friends with all the other girls who made cheerleader. It felt like in one moment I'd lost both my best friend and the thing I'd wanted most.

But I put a smile on my face and did my best to act like I didn't really care. I tried out for the dance team and made it in spite of my limited rhythm, and I pretended that I preferred the dance team anyway. Becky and I went on as if everything was fine, and on the surface it was. But I'd let envy creep in, and nothing will erode the foundation of a friendship quite like the resentment that builds from wanting what someone else has without even factoring in that maybe you have something they want as well. We become blind to our own blessings and the gifts God has given us when we're focused on the things we don't have, but I didn't learn that lesson until many years later. Or maybe just last year. Or maybe I have to continually remind myself even now.

In spite of how I may have felt inwardly, I did my best to get over it because I loved Becky and didn't want us to grow apart. Our friendship continued, and we still spent as much time together as possible the summer before our senior year began. In fact, it was that summer when I got into what still stands as a legendary amount of trouble during my high school years.

For some reason, Becky's parents were out of town one weekend, and I begged my mom to let me spend the night at Becky's house. After all, I was going to be in college in just one year, and she needed to TRUST ME. I was responsible and capable of making good decisions. Yes. Technically I was capable of making good decisions—just not necessarily smart enough to choose them. Which is why Becky and I decided we needed to sneak out to attend a SigEp party at the local college that Saturday night.

We had it all planned out. We'd call my mom at 10:30 and lie that we were in for the night, and then we'd leave the phone off the hook in case she called back. Naturally she'd just assume we were talking to our friends on the phone and never bother to actually check in on us. What could possibly go wrong?

(Obviously, this was before the days of cell phones and all other forms of social media, for which I am forever grateful. The only photographic evidence of my high school stupidity and poor fashion choices resides safely between the pages of a few puffy paint–covered photo albums and not on the Internet for parental eyes and future employers to see.)

So we called my mom and did the check-in, sprayed and teased our hair with copious amounts of Aussie Sprunch Spray, put on our best outfits from the Limited, and headed out to the SigEp house for a night of fun and frivolity. Any fear I had over this ill-advised adventure immediately dissipated when I saw a college boy I'd had a crush on for years making his way to talk to me. The truth is, there were a lot of other high school kids there besides us who obviously lived under more benevolent, lenient regimes than Becky and I did, so the whole night was spectacular. We felt so grown up at this fraternity party as we mingled with friends, new and old, and time got away from us until the last keg was floated and we realized it was 1 a.m.

But Becky and I weren't ready for the party to be over. So, in what still stands as one of the dumbest decisions I've ever made, we invited a large group of the SigEp party attendees to follow us back to Becky's house to continue the festivities. And I don't mean four or five people. I'm talking in the neighborhood of twenty to thirty people who then spread the good news like wildfire to fifty or sixty other people. Becky loaded up her car with a few partygoers, and I took the opportunity to jump into the Mustang convertible that belonged to the boy I had a crush on as we made the fifteen-minute journey back to Becky's house on the other side of town.

Fortunately (and I'm using that word loosely), Becky made it back to her house about five minutes before I did and hung up the phone we'd left off the receiver all those hours ago, only to have it ring immediately. My mother was on the line, demanding to know where we'd been and what was going on. And my mom didn't buy that we'd been safely at home all that time talking on the phone, mainly because she'd already driven by the house and knew that wasn't the case. So as I pulled up to Becky's house with the college boy I was trying to impress, Becky came flying out the front door like a modern-day Paul Revere shouting, "YOUR MOM IS COMING! YOUR MOM IS COMING!" which is all it took for me to go from pseudo-sophisticated college-girl wannabe to a sixteen-year-old chicken with her head cut off. I jumped out of the Mustang and told the boy he needed to leave the premises IMMEDIATELY and then scrambled into Becky's house to change out of my Limited outfit into pajamas and scrub the makeup off my face, while Becky explained that she'd told my mom we'd been driving around in search of an open grocery store to buy root beer so we could make ice-cream floats.

Can we discuss for a moment how this signifies one of the reasons Becky was my best friend? How calm and cool is that answer? I mean, no, it wasn't believable for one second, but you have to admire a girl who can come up with anything other than sheer panic when faced with the prospect of a firing squad. We were just two innocent high school girls being falsely accused of shenanigans when all we wanted was a simple root beer float.

Just about the time I quit hyperventilating, I heard my mom's car pull up in the driveway. I walked out to meet her only to discover that it wasn't just my mom in the car but also my little sister AND my grandmother. You know what will flat shut down any remaining vestiges of coolness? When you're busted by multiple generations of your family.

My mom told Becky and me to lock up the house and get in her car because we were going back to my house RIGHT THIS MINUTE. And we did what we were told because you don't mess with someone who has seen completely and totally through your barrage of lies. But what I had completely forgotten in all the panic and desperation of the previous ten minutes was that we had a whole passel of partygoers on their way to Becky's house, and the first one turned into her driveway as we were pulling out.

"Who is that?" my mom asked suspiciously.

"I have no idea," I replied, which was technically the truth.

Maybe it was someone who had heard we'd found some elusive root beer at a grocery store across town and decided they, too, needed to partake of a root beer float.

As we drove down Becky's block, two perps in the back of a Honda Accord with my little sister sitting between us, a line of about twenty cars began to turn onto the street. I felt my face grow hot just watching it all play out. It was two o'clock in the morning, Becky didn't live on a busy street, and our story was getting flimsier by the minute. But we continued to profess that we had no idea why there appeared to be a traffic jam until my mom turned the car around and pulled back into Becky's driveway just as a drunken fraternity boy stumbled up to her car window and asked, "Is this where the party is?"

Well.

So this is how my life ends.

That's when I discovered that there is such a thing as "inevitable consequences." It was early July, and I spent the next month completely and totally grounded, which was actually a relief since my original sentence had been for the rest of the summer. My only respite was early morning dance team practice, but I was to come straight home afterward. Do not pass go; do not collect two hundred dollars; do not at any time appear to be happy or carefree. However, for reasons I still don't completely understand, Becky's punishment wasn't nearly as severe. Maybe it was because her mom subscribed to the belief that "teenagers will be teenagers," or maybe it was because she didn't have to drive all over town at two o'clock in the morning with her own mother and small child in the car looking for a bunch of juvenile delinquents. All I know is that I was banished to social purgatory while Becky was free to enjoy her summer, and I was a little bitter about it.

(Of course, now that I'm a mother, I have to say that being grounded for a month seems fairly lenient for this series of offenses. Caroline would be on her way to military school. Or a convent.)

Looking back, this was one more crack in the fault line that had formed in my friendship with Becky. All those little things seem so small now, but in the currency of our teenage economy, something in the dynamic shifted, and eventually our relationship felt more like a competition than a friendship. And the final blow was on its way.

In early August my prison sentence was finally lifted, and I was free to reengage in my social life, albeit with the limits that come when parents have been burned by believing their daughter is smart enough to not sneak out at night to attend a fraternity party. In an attempt to prove that I was indeed remorseful and filled with sorrow for my crimes, I'd spent the previous month attending church on a regular basis. The truth is, that was one of very few social options I had that didn't include going to my grandparents' house or driving my sister around town, so I took advantage of it. And my religious ways paid off, because I caught the eye of a very cute college boy who was home for the summer. He'd asked me out a few times while I was grounded (Oh, the mortification of having to turn down a date with a college boy by informing him that you're grounded. I might as well have had to say I was still being potty trained.), and we finally had our first date one night after I was free to live again.

Over the next few weeks we went out several times and enjoyed being together. Neither of us was under any illusion that this was anything serious, because he was heading back to school in less than a month, and we weren't really invested enough to think about a long-distance relationship. But we had fun, and I invited Becky to tag along with us on many of our outings.

There was one night when we were all out together, and my boyfriend and Becky had to drop me off first because my curfew was still significantly altered after the escapades of the summer. I didn't think anything of it until the next day, when I went to spend the night at Becky's house. I walked into her bedroom to set my stuff down and noticed her journal lying open on her bed. Here's where I admit I shouldn't have looked at it. But I did. And that's when curiosity killed both the cat and our friendship in one fell swoop, because what I saw was her written admission that the night before, she'd kissed the boy I was dating. I was furious, and I was hurt. I grabbed my stuff and stormed out of her house, vowing to never speak to her again.

Here's the thing. I had a right to be angry. It was a betrayal. Yet when I think back on what hurt the most, I realize that it wasn't really about the boy at all but the fact that he was one more thing in a long line of things that had gone her way and not mine. It took me many years to see that it wasn't so much the betrayal that broke our friendship, but the jealousy. I think most relationships that end have died a thousand little deaths and not so much one big one.

I look back on that time with so much regret over how I handled the situation. I cut off my friendship with Becky and missed out on spending my senior year of high school with the girl who'd been everything to me for two years. And it wasn't that I didn't have other really great friends to hang out with—I absolutely did, and a few of them are still close friends, even though we see one another on Facebook more often than in real life these days. But there are a few people in your life who become so much a part of you that it feels like you're missing a limb when they're gone. That's what Becky was to me. I spent my senior year looking fine on the outside but grieving the loss on the inside. I wish I could go back and tell my seventeen-year-old self, "Buck up, Francis. Get over yourself. None of this is worth losing a friend."

Eventually Becky and I did find our way back to each other, but it was never the same as it was back then. We were both more guarded, a little more cautious with our hearts. And ultimately, the only way to immerse yourself in true, deep friendship is to be willing to jump in with both feet, arms wide open, for whatever will be. We didn't get back to that place. Our lives went in different directions, and we made new friends and had new adventures that didn't include each other.

But our friendship, both the good and the bad, taught me so many important lessons about what it means to be a friend. There is no achievement so great—even becoming a high school cheerleader—that it's worth losing a friend over. For every thing you may envy about a friend, she probably has an equal number of things she could envy about you. And while it's been said that comparison is the thief of joy, I'll add that it can also be a destroyer of relationships.

When I returned Becky's call a few years ago, after my mother-in-law had relayed the message to me, I learned that she had called to let me know she was getting a divorce and was, understandably, devastated about it. The phone call wasn't really about Becky wanting to tell me the news before I heard it from someone else as much as it was that she needed a friend. At a time when she was being crushed with such a heavy burden, she needed someone to listen.

And in spite of all the years that had passed, it somehow made sense that she called me. She and her ex-husband lived in our hometown and most of their friends knew them as a couple, but she knew that I would be on her side and do my best to help her through, even after all the water that had passed under our respective bridges. I can't tell you what it meant to me—what it still means to me—that she chose to call me. We went through so much together during our teen years, and I've often looked back on that time and wished I'd been a better friend. Those are the years when we tend to be so wrapped up in ourselves and are still learning that the world doesn't revolve around us. I knew that Becky and I loved each other, but we'd also hurt each other. Through that phone call, though, any lingering doubts I had about our friendship melted away. All she wanted was someone to help her through her pain, and all I wanted was to make her pain go away. Ultimately, that's one of the cornerstones of friendship.

And I think it speaks to how much you change and grow over the years that not only did Becky feel safe calling me that day, but also that all I felt for her was deep sadness. I took no joy in her pain. She talked, I listened, we laughed, and we cried. The years and the distance melted away, and we were almost like those two high school girls again, but with a little more wisdom and a lot more grace. And grateful for another chance to love each other again.

CHAPTER 6

The Knitting of Souls

Friendship is unnecessary, like philosophy, like art. . . . It has no survival value; rather it is one of those things which give value to survival.

C. S. LEWIS

THERE ARE PEOPLE who believe that college football is just a game. And to those people I say . . . well, I don't say much, because we don't have anything in common.

At some point during my high school years, I decided I wanted to go to Texas A&M. We didn't have family ties to the school or anything like that; it just seemed like a good choice for reasons I can't even remember now. Then I went to visit the campus at the beginning of my senior year in high school, and that sealed the deal. I'll never forget watching an introductory film called *The Spirit of Aggieland* before taking a campus tour and getting chills at the legacy of spirit and heart and tradition.

My point is that I have loved Aggie football for a long time now. Throughout all these years I've experienced some major football highs: Aaron Wallace holding up Andre Ware's helmet as we shocked the University of Houston, destroying Ty Detmer and BYU in the 1990 Holiday Bowl, the 1998 Big 12 championship game when we beat Kansas State, the emotional win over the Longhorns after the Aggie Bonfire collapsed in '99, and beating number-one-ranked Oklahoma in 2002 at Kyle Field.

I have jumped up and down and cheered and yelled until I've lost my voice. I've said words you'll never hear in Sunday school and probably let way too many of my Saturday-evening moods be determined by how well (or how badly) the Aggies played. There have been countless times when Perry has had to tell me to TAKE IT DOWN A NOTCH, GLADYS.

Because there have also been some serious lows. Standing in the freezing cold with my best friends at the Cotton Bowl in '91 as we watched the Aggies lose 10–2 to Florida State and shared one hot dog since we'd spent all our money the night before, celebrating New Year's Eve in Dallas, because college kids are smart. Then doing the same thing the next year, but watching us lose to Notre Dame that time. And the next year, losing to Notre Dame again. And basically the entire Dennis Franchione era.

But my love for the Aggies has never wavered.

Because it's about so much more than just football. Texas A&M gave me some of the best memories of my life. I arrived there as a scared eighteen-year-old way back in ye olden days of 1989 and left in 1994 (shout-out for a victory lap and an extra football season) with memories I'll have forever. To this day, most of my closest friends are the people I met while I was there. Being an Aggie has left an imprint on my life forever in all the best ways.

So that's why I love the Aggies. And that's why I love Aggie football. It has been more than twenty years of throwing cotton on the field and wearing cotton in my gold hoop earrings. Being an

Aggie means yelling until I'm hoarse and freaking out and getting tears in my eyes every time I hear the announcer say, "Now forming at the north end of Kyle Field, the nationally famous Fightin' Texas Aggie Band" while the crowd goes wild. It means getting a job at the ticket office with your best friend when you're a student so you can get fifty-yard-line seats to every game. It means reading all the message boards and tailgating and following every step of recruitment to see which high school players will decide to play at A&M. Like our school song says, "There's a spirit that can ne'er be told."

All that to say, when the Aggies walked into Bryant-Denny Stadium in the fall of 2012 against the University of Alabama, whose team was ranked number one in the nation, and walked out of there with one of the biggest victories in Aggie football history, it was a momentous day.

Gulley and I have a long-standing tradition that involves watching every game we can at her house. It's a system that works for us, and we usually don't invite other people besides family to join us, because we tend to be a little intense. I may or may not have moments when I need to put my head between my knees to keep from passing out. We eat chips and dips, and we pace and yell and scream and offer deep, insightful football analysis to the coaches on the sidelines. You know, just in case they're looking for advice from two middle-aged women.

By the third quarter of that game against Alabama, my stomach was in knots. I stood up. I sat down. I paced. Gulley and I told the kids to quit eating their chips so loudly. We may have permanently scarred the dog. Gulley's dad called at one point to tell us he got a cramp in his foot during the third quarter and was worried he was having a stroke from the stress. And frankly, we'd been worried about the same thing. The human body can only take so much.

When it finally came down to Alabama's fourth and goal, and the Alabama quarterback, AJ McCarron, threw an interception, I'm pretty sure I blacked out for a good three seconds. And I'm not even going to lie: Gulley and I jumped up and down until we wet our pants. That's the downside of being a fanatic football fan when you're a woman over forty who has had a child. But it didn't even matter, because all we cared about at that moment was that the Aggies had beaten Alabama.

It was a golden day. There have been other victories, but after a year of hearing that the Aggies weren't ready for the SEC, and that they were going to be like a lamb going to the slaughter, it felt like vindication.

Which is why, immediately after we counted off the last ten seconds of the game, Gulley and I loaded up the kids in my station wagon, grabbed Gulley's Aggie flag, and made several victory laps around the neighborhood honking "The Aggie War Hymn."

I have always been proud to be an Aggie, and I've always loved watching Aggie football with Gulley, but maybe never more so than on that day.

By the time I graduated from high school, I was ready for a fresh start and eager to meet new people. Texas A&M has a great thing called Fish Camp every summer before students start their freshman year. It's essentially a three-day camp where you meet other freshmen as well as the upperclassmen who serve as counselors. This is where the newbies are fully indoctrinated into all Texas A&M culture and traditions and are convinced that, without a doubt, Texas A&M is the best school in the world.

In fact, I had such a great time at Fish Camp that I called my high school boyfriend from a pay phone and broke up with him while I was there. Yes, we ended up getting back together, which led to my bad decision to transfer to another school for the spring semester, but for one brief, shining moment, being immersed in the full Aggie experience made me brave.

(For those of you born after 1985, a pay phone was a communication device that required you to use a quarter to make a phone call. And in addition, it made you wish you carried rubbing alcohol in your purse to wipe off the receiver because EW about all the people who'd used it before you.)

So after a freshman year filled with turmoil (please see chapter 1 for more on boyfriend angst, dubious decisions to leave the holy ground of College Station, and desperate phone calls to my college patron, aka my dad), I was excited to be back at the school I loved. And it was this enthusiasm that caused me to throw myself fully into the college experience. This was both good, in that I joined a sorority and made new friends, and bad, in that I also discovered nickel beer night and the joys of late-night queso and chips from Taco Cabana.

One night as I was leaving the sorority house after a pledge meeting, I noticed that one of the older girls had a bumper sticker on her car that said, "Diamond Darlings." It piqued my interest because I am a fan of both diamonds and things that are darling. So the next time I saw her, she explained what it was, and that's how I ended up deciding it was something I wanted to do. I already had a feeling that sorority life wasn't going to be my favorite because there were requirements like structured study hours, whereas I could easily picture myself spending a lot of time watching baseball. It's funny how that one seemingly insignificant decision led to so much more than I could have imagined. Sometimes you can look back on times in your life and know that God was guiding you even when you didn't know you were supposed to be listening.

Which brings us back to Gulley.

So let's start with the fact that Gulley isn't her real name. It's Amy. But we are children of the '70s, which means that we were friends with approximately 4,073 Amys in college, and thus we called them all by their last names instead of their first, and Gulley is her maiden name.

It was always Gulley's preference to be called by her last name, because she contends there is nothing worse than being known as "the other Amy." That being "the other Amy" is basically the equivalent of someone saying, "This is the Amy I don't like as much as the additional Amys in my life."

All these years later, she is still Gulley to me, because I'd already called her that for almost ten years before she got married. It's like when my cousin Terri decided she wanted to be called Jill when she was eighteen years old, and the whole family just called her Terri Jill from that point on because if people referenced Jill, nobody knew who they were talking about. Or maybe it's how Prince's friends felt when he changed his name to that symbol back in the '90s. Except I bet they felt like he needed to get over himself with his tricky symbol name. It's a different thing to get married and have a legitimate name change than it is to decide on a name that people have to draw.

Gulley's married name is Fisher. So yes. Her name is now Amy Fisher. And woe to you if you make a Joey Buttafuoco joke in her presence. Any reference to "Long Island Lolita" will be met with a withering stare and possibly a dry, sarcastic, "Wow, you're the first person who's ever made that joke." I'm just warning you. Almost nothing makes her angry, and she has one of the longest fuses of anyone I know, but this is where she draws the line.

The Christmas formal where Gulley and I sat beside each other with our bad dates proved to be just the beginning of our friendship. We went our separate ways for Christmas break, but when we came back to school for the spring semester, we jumped right into baseball season. I'd also like to say we jumped right back into our academic pursuits, but that would be a complete falsehood, and I don't want you to labor under any delusions that I really saw college as an opportunity to learn more about things like biology and history. And I have to say in hindsight that I was correct. You absolutely learn a lot of things during your four—or five—years of college, but I've found that the vast majority of useful life lessons occur outside the classroom. How else would I have learned that drinking four Big Gulps of Coke from 7-Eleven each day might cause you to put on excessive weight due to the fact that you're consuming an extra two thousand calories a day in beverages alone?

The beginning of baseball season meant that Gulley and I were together all the time. There were about four games a week, and we were required to be at the majority of them—not that it needed to be mandatory, because there was nowhere else we'd rather be. We spent more time at the baseball fields than anywhere else, and we loved every minute of it.

Then there were the road trips. This was back in the days of the old Southwest Conference, so there were trips to Rice, Baylor, TCU, and the evil empire in Austin.

(I'm just kidding about the evil empire.)

(Kind of.)

It was our road trip to TCU that proved to be one of the

moments that sealed my friendship with Gulley forever. Eight of us loaded up in two cars and caravanned to Fort Worth for the games and, equally important, a trip to Billy Bob's, otherwise known as the world's largest honky-tonk, because wouldn't you go to the world's largest honky-tonk if you had the opportunity? Truth be told, I'd been dying to go to a real-live honky-tonk ever since I'd seen John Travolta ride that mechanical bull at Gilley's in *Urban Cowboy*.

I will never forget the experience, because that was the night I learned that the mechanical bull experience might be all for naught if you die from secondhand cigarette smoke inhalation while waiting in line. I'm starting to cough just thinking about it. It was also the first time a boy flipped me upside down while we were two-stepping across the dance floor. This makes it sound like I'm a much more proficient dancer than I am. The truth is, I was more than a little taken aback by this sequence of events. Sometimes a girl needs some warning if her dance partner is about to assume she's Nadia Comaneci.

My friend Jen grew up in the Dallas area, so she not only invited us to stay at her dad's house for the weekend but also volunteered his Suburban as our official vehicle for driving all over the Dallas/ Fort Worth area. What she neglected to mention was that her dad had a prosthetic leg and kept an extra in the back seat. You know what will make some college girls come unhinged? The sight of a leg not attached to a person in the backseat of a Suburban.

When we arrived at Jen's dad's house late Friday night after the first baseball game, everyone began to sort out who was going to sleep where, and it became apparent that there weren't enough beds for everyone. This is the kind of attention to detail that college girls lack when playing hostess.

So without even thinking twice about it, Gulley and I declared that we were happy to share a twin bed for the weekend. And here's the thing: I meant it. I feel that you can't fully appreciate the momentous nature of this unless I make you aware of my myriad sleep issues. I need about six pillows at all times, the temperature has to be just right, and the sheets have to be pulled tight and preferably made out of a cotton that would make angel wings jealous of the sheer softness. You know that episode of *Friends* when Joey Tribbiani declares, "Joey doesn't share food"? That's me. Except with a bed. Even after seventeen years of marriage, my husband and I sleep under different sets of covers, as far apart as possible. It's very romantic.

But I was willing to share a twin bed with Gulley. We climbed into that bed and spent the rest of the night not even pretending to sleep but instead laughing and whispering as we shared stories about our families, our ex-boyfriends, and the experiences that were shaping the women we were trying to become at nineteen years old. I look back on that weekend as the weekend I knew I'd found a kindred spirit.

You hear so many people talk about finding their soul mates only in relation to who they marry, but I think that, as women, our real soul mates are often found when we recognize some version of ourselves in someone else. Gulley and I were both children of divorce; we knew what it was like to be shuttled back and forth on weekends and all the emotional land mines that lie therein. We had been hurt by girl friends we'd trusted. We found humor in the same quirky things and shared a love of novelty rap songs.

Maybe it's where we were in life at that time, with the wide-eyed innocence of girls on the brink of adulthood, but we were vulnerable with each other in that way you are when you know you've found someone you can completely trust with your heart. It was like each of us went into the friendship with an awareness of how the other had been hurt and disappointed in the past, and there was an unspoken vow that we would do our best to see that we never caused each other any pain. We saw each other's fragility masked in a brave exterior and began to make each other stronger people than we'd been before.

I've loved the Bible story about the friendship between Jonathan and David ever since the days when I learned about it on the flannel board in Sunday school, but when I read it as an adult, I noticed that it says in 1 Samuel 18:1, "The soul of Jonathan was knit to the soul of David, and Jonathan loved him as his own soul" (ESV). That's a powerful bond. It's clear that Jonathan didn't work to knit his soul to David's, but that God absolutely showed up in that moment to forever knit their hearts and souls together. What God knew at that moment—which neither Jonathan nor David could have envisioned—was how much they would need each other in the years to come. God brought them together at a point when he knew they would both serve to make the other a stronger man than they would have been alone.

Having your soul knit to another isn't for the faint of heart. It means you bear your own hurts along with those of your friend. You cry when she cries and laugh when she laughs and come up with plots to kill someone who causes her any pain. You love harder, laugh louder, live richer, and become more together than you could ever be by yourself. Soul knitting is putting your heart and your name in the hands of another person and saying, "I trust you with all of this" and having that person do the same.

Here's a little-known fact about Gulley and me. We were delivered by the same doctor at the same hospital in Houston, Texas, almost exactly one year apart. For the next eighteen years, our lives took twists and turns and moved us in all kinds of directions, but I believe that God always knew he was going to bring us together at exactly the time we'd need each other the most, and it would be his gift to us for the rest of our lives. That's real friendship.

And I also think he had to laugh knowing that for all the sweet, tender moments we'd share, we had a lot of dumb in us that was bound to come out along the way.

After that trip to TCU and the sharing of the twin bed, I knew that Gulley was one of my people. In fact, I trusted her so much that I called her on the phone one morning and asked her to lie for me.

It's true. I'm a terrible, horrible person.

But let's please remember that I was a nineteen-year-old girl with a propensity for drama and absolutely not a lick of good sense. Case in point: I was taking Japanese for my foreign-language requirement. This was not a point in my life where I was aware of my strengths and weaknesses, nor did I have a good grasp of reality. In what universe was I ever going to have an opportunity to compliment the people of Japan on their lovely cherry trees?

I had been dating a boy for most of the year (Yes. I dated a lot of boys. See "weakness" mentioned above.), but I began to notice another boy who also began to notice me. Yet I was not a secure enough person to break up with Boy A to date Boy B. I wanted to see if Boy B was going to work out before I gave up Boy A.

(I can't believe I'm telling this story. Did I mention I'm a terrible person?)

My brilliant decision to date two boys at once worked really well until I couldn't account for where I'd been one evening when Boy A decided to surprise me at my apartment. So I opted to tell him that I'd been out at Gulley's parents' house studying with Gulley, because it felt like a story he couldn't really confirm. But then I got paranoid that he might try to confirm it, so I called Gulley, explained the whole story, and asked if she'd cover for me. Without missing a beat, and with no judgment whatsoever, she said, "Sure!"

And then I loved her even more when Boy A and I happened to see her on campus a few days later and she said, "I had such a great time studying with you the other night!"

See what she did there? Gulley went above and beyond. Yes, it was terrible, but I knew then that she was solid gold.

We've always said our friendship was cemented when she covered me without a single question, and we've been covering for each other ever since.

(Now that I've confessed to my duplicitous ways, I need you to please remember that it happened twenty-four years ago, and that I just talked about David and Jonathan from THE BIBLE a few paragraphs ago.)

Anyway, I eventually broke up with Boy A and then proceeded to get dumped by Boy B. So Justin Timberlake is right when he says that what goes around comes all the way back around. He's also right about the importance of a pocket full of soul, but that's neither here nor there and really doesn't apply to this story at all.

CHAPTER 7

The Fantastic Four

*When you're in jail, a good friend will be trying to bail you out. A best
friend will be in the cell next to you saying, "D---, that was fun."*

GROUCHO MARX

I BELIEVE I MENTIONED earlier that my daughter, Caroline, has just
started junior high. In our school district there are two elementary schools that come together to make up the junior high student body, and this past summer there were all sorts of playdates
planned by various mothers to help their daughters get to know
some of the girls they'd be going to school with in the fall. This
is all well and good, but it was largely the mothers who planned
these things based on the other mothers they liked and not necessarily who their daughters might enjoy.

And I understand the thinking behind it, but it also made me
wonder what happened to the good ol' days when kids just went to
school and became friends with the kid they sat next to in science
class, with no parental involvement whatsoever. Do you know

what moms of the '70s didn't concern themselves with? Their children's social lives. I mean, sure, my mom would eventually meet the mother of one of my friends if she became someone I spent a lot of time with, but there were no organized playdates and strategies to help me make friends. Back then, moms considered good mothering to be remembering to crack the station wagon windows while they smoked their Virginia Slims and we rolled around in the back with nary a car seat nor a seat belt to be found, before going home to eat gluten-filled pasta out of a can.

One thing I've learned over the years is that you figure out who your people are fairly quickly in any type of social setting. That's not to say you don't enjoy the other people who are around, but there are just certain people who capture part of your heart in a particular way—maybe because of shared interests and common values, but also because there's something deeper in you that calls out to each other like a lighthouse beacon showing you the way home.

That's what happened that first spring of Diamond Darlings. As the semester went on, I found myself spending more and more time with Gulley, Jen, and Tiffany. Jen was the girl in the denim wrap skirt who had breezed into that first meeting with so much bravado that I found her intimidating, but since she was a freshman who lived in the dorms, and I was a very sophisticated college sophomore living in an apartment, I mustered up my courage to invite her over for dinner one night when she mentioned she was craving a home-cooked meal. I won her over with my fabulous chicken stir-fry. I like to say it's because my cooking was so phenomenal, but the truth was she was starving for anything that didn't come from the campus cafeteria or McDonald's, and she ate it like it was her last meal. I think I had to microwave an additional two cups of rice to make sure we had enough. My Italian grandmother, Me-Ma, would be so proud to know that I've followed her example of using food to draw people in.

Then Tiff. How do I describe Tiff? She is one of the sweetest human beings you could ever meet. An absolute beauty queen with a heart of solid gold. Tiff is the one who makes everyone's head turn when she walks in with her blinding smile and blonde hair. You kind of want to hate her for being so effortlessly gorgeous, but then you talk to her for five seconds and fall in love. One of the first conversations we ever had was when we were sitting outside a baseball dugout, and I asked what she was majoring in. (A fail-safe conversation starter for all college kids who are introverts but don't really know it yet.)

She looked at me and said without blinking, "Sports management. But all I really want to do is get married and have kids."

I adored her instantly, because I secretly wanted the exact same thing but wasn't yet at a point in my life where I felt secure enough to say it out loud. I admired that she was who she was with no apologies.

It didn't take long before the four of us completely let down our guards and allowed one another to see the depth and breadth of our real selves. We were inseparable and despondent at the thought of having to part ways for the summer. Fortunately for us, the Aggies ended up hosting the Southwest Conference baseball tournament that year, which delayed the inevitable because we had to stay in town to work the games. We had all given up our apartments and dorm rooms at that point, so we spent every night at Gulley's parents' house and chose to make one big pallet on the living room floor so we could all sleep piled in together. None of us dared to leave the room to sleep in an actual bed, lest we miss out on something funny.

And we thought *everything* was funny. That's what I remember most about that time; I had never laughed that much. Tiff in particular would make us laugh, even when she didn't mean to, with declarations like, "I was starving, and then I remembered I didn't eat lunch. So I swallowed my gum, and now I feel full." Apparently she was on a supermodel diet before we even knew what that was.

I was the queen of trivia (a trait I still possess today, much to the delight of everyone who knows me—except maybe the opposite of that) and constantly shared such tips as "Jalapeños increase your metabolism" and "Lotion gets rid of cellulite." Sadly, I'm not sure either of these held true for us, probably because we all ate diets that largely consisted of shrimp Caesar salads from Chili's, but it was worth a shot.

Gulley tended to say what everyone else was thinking but wouldn't actually say out loud, and Jen was pretty much like our camp director, making sure we were all where we were supposed to be and doing what we were supposed to be doing. She offered unsolicited advice on everything, from how much we should tip the waitress at Sonic to the number of hours we should be studying in order to maintain a decent grade point average to the fact she found it socially unacceptable to order a chicken-fried steak in public.

We all had our strengths and weaknesses and unique personalities, and in some ways were all so different (See chicken-fried steak reference above. I've never been one to turn it down in public or in private.), but there was something that drew us together and forged a bond that still exists to this day. We may not all live in the same town, and our lives have all gone in different directions, but we all know who to call when bad times come and we need a friend. I know this to be true because we've lived it out as the years have gone by.

Ecclesiastes 4:12 says that "a cord of three strands is not quickly broken," but I would maintain that the same applies to a cord of four strands. The four of us became inextricably linked by some incorporeal bond. I know that sometimes it gets complicated when a group of women become friends, but we seemed to capture that bit of lightning in a bottle in that we all just fit together. Individually, we couldn't have been more different, but together our personalities all dovetailed in a way that made all of us better people than we were by ourselves. There was no jealousy or competition or insecurity—just love for one another and what each person brought to the friendship. Back then, I had no idea how rare a gift I'd been given in each of them.

You can imagine how thrilled we were when the baseball team won their tournament and advanced to the regional tournament at LSU in Baton Rouge. Louisiana? Road trip? Um. Yes, please.

We convinced Gulley's dad that her Pontiac Sunbird probably wasn't reliable enough for the six-hour trip, and he agreed to let us take his red Chevy Blazer, complete with a car phone. This was back in the days when car phones were truly phones in the car, which were attached to a bag that I guess held all the technological components you needed in order to participate in calling someone from the car. It basically made us feel like the Jetsons, and I regret to inform you that we later learned that each phone call we made from that car phone cost Gulley's dad approximately $315. And unfortunately, we'd felt the need to call A LOT of people just to say, "Hey! We're calling you from THE CAR!"

We loaded ourselves into the Blazer wearing our finest wind shorts, with sliding shorts underneath, along with our K-Swiss tennis shoes and scrunched-down ankle socks. We blasted C+C Music Factory and sang "Everybody Dance Now" all the way down I-10 as we made our way to Baton Rouge, stopping occasionally for nutritional staples such as Corn Nuts, Big Gulps of Coke, and chocolate Zingers. As we talked and laughed and told stories and created our own little world of inside jokes and words and phrases only we understood, I had a feeling that life couldn't get much better.

Along the way we learned that Tiff was about to break up with her longtime boyfriend; Jen's dad was in worse health than we'd realized, and she was facing losing him at an early age; Gulley was struggling to break out of a pattern of worrying too much about what other people thought; and I had a tendency to get carsick if I wasn't driving the car. I also tended to get a little militant about what justifies a bathroom stop, and I will tell you, it doesn't involve stopping every thirty minutes.

We arrived in Baton Rouge to pouring rain and baseball games that were constantly being postponed due to the weather. But we didn't care. We spent a week at the Courtyard Marriott, all crammed into one small room, and we would have been happy to stay that way forever. We played poker late into the night, chased one another down the hallways, and hung out by the pool when the weather allowed and we weren't at the baseball fields. When the Aggies lost their second game and were eliminated from the tournament, we were sad to see it all come to an end.

And so we went our separate ways for the summer. Gulley went home to nearby Bryan, Jen had a job working as a waitress in Dallas, Tiff went to Wichita to be with her family, and I ended up in Houston at my dad's house, where I enjoyed a brief stint as a hostess at Ninfa's Mexican Restaurant. This was practically back in the days of the Pony Express, and since long-distance calls were so expensive, we talked on the phone only occasionally. But we did send a constant stream of letters and cards updating one another on our summer activities. Gulley and I managed to visit each other several times because we lived only an hour and a half apart.

It was on one of my visits to stay with Gulley at her parents' house in Bryan that we decided it might be fun to swim in all the fountains on the Texas A&M campus. This is the kind of idea that would cause my current self to question the bacteria levels of water in public fountains, but I was still a developing germaphobe back in 1991, so I thought this was a spectacular plan. The only snag was that Gulley had recently had a wart frozen off the bottom of her foot and wasn't supposed to get her foot wet. Of course, she didn't tell people about the wart because that's the sort of ailment college girls find beyond embarrassing, and she chose instead to concoct a tale about stepping on a hot coal on the Fourth of July. Which is totally plausible, because how many times have you been at an Independence Day gathering where hot coals are randomly scattered around the yard?

Anyway, Gulley couldn't get her foot wet, so instead of the practical decision to maybe not swim in bacteria-laden fountains, we decided to procure a Mrs. Baird's plastic bread bag to put over her foot and then secured the whole thing with at least half a roll of duct tape. I believe this is known as medical improvisation. Or maybe a starter kit for a guide titled *So You Want to Be a Backwoods Physician*.

At the end of the spring semester, Tiff, Jen, Gulley, and I had all lamented that we'd already committed to various living arrangements for the following year. We *really* wanted to share an apartment together, but we didn't feel like we could back out of our existing plans. Well, that is until Jen called me during the summer to tell me that her plans had fallen through and asked if I wanted to share an apartment with her and a friend of hers from high school. This was exactly what I wanted to do, and I immediately decided to bail on my plans to live in the sorority house. The only problem was that the sorority threatened to sue me when I informed them I'd changed my mind. You know what will make you rethink your commitment to Greek sisterhood? The threat of a lawsuit.

Fortunately, my dad has a friend who specializes in real estate law, and he informed us that the sorority didn't actually have grounds to sue me. Which is a shame, because that would have been a lucrative lawsuit for them, what with the zeros of dollars I had to my name, along with my Adrienne Vittadini wardrobe and my 1985 Honda CR-X. However, all these years later my dad still likes to talk about that time I almost got us sued by a sorority, because he's hilarious.

So in the fall of '91 I moved into a truly subpar apartment complex with Jen and her friend from high school. They were sharing a room, which technically meant I had my own room, except that Gulley was still living in a dorm and quickly became my unofficial roommate. It made so much more sense for her to just stay at our apartment than to drive home late every night.

(You should also know that we referred to the dorm as "the D" because we worried that "the dorm" sounded way too nerdy.)

(This is the kind of thing that seemed really important back then.)

The upside was that Gulley still had her parking pass for the dorm garage on campus, which proved to be the only reason any of us ever made it to class on time.

Tiff, Jen, Gulley, and I were so happy to be back together, and we didn't miss a beat as we dove back into spending all our time together—occasionally studying for a class, but more often than not looking for social opportunities.

It was later that fall that the University of Southwestern Louisiana Ragin' Cajun football team was coming to play the Aggies at Kyle Field. This was back in the early '90s heyday of Aggie football glory, so everyone knew that the Ragin' Cajuns didn't have a prayer of beating us. It was a magical time. And not that most of you care, but I'll have you know that we never lost a home football game during all five of my college years.

The Monday before the game, I was sitting in class avidly listening to a fascinating lecture about the ins and outs of political science and taking furious notes about libel being a tort. . . . I'm totally kidding—I was reading our student newspaper, *The Battalion*, while the professor gave his lecture. This is just further evidence of what a conscientious student I was, along with the fact that when my dad came to visit me earlier that fall, I pointed to the completely wrong building and announced that it was the library. And because he loves me, he kept paying my tuition anyway.

So I was reading the newspaper when I noticed an open letter to the student body from a professor named Dr. Abraham at USL, Home of the Ragin' Cajuns. The letter was hysterical, and I wish I had a copy now, but it was basically an invitation for a select number of Aggie students to join him and some other Ragin' Cajuns for a pregame tailgate party, complete with complimentary Cajun-style food and drink. He said that the first twenty or so people to call him would be invited, and he included his phone number.

I left class immediately and sped home to tell the girls about it and see if they were interested in going. We called Dr. Abraham and left a message informing him that we had seen his letter and would love to join them for the tailgate party and, by the way, we were Diamond Darlings for the baseball team. Gulley and I thought this fact might give us an edge, and I am embarrassed to admit that we probably said it with an air of importance normally reserved for statements like "I'm an ambassador to China, and in my spare time I volunteer in orphanages."

He called us back, said we were in, and told us to show up on Saturday on the George Bush Drive side of Kyle Field and to bring our appetites. He wasn't kidding.

We showed up at eleven on Saturday morning, and the beer and crawfish were already flowing. They had enough food to feed the entire stadium. It was a true Cajun feast—boudin, crawfish, and sausage were plentiful. The USL fans were the nicest people imaginable, as you would expect from a group of people who invited the competition to a tailgate party using the student newspaper, and we had the best time sitting around listening to their stories. (Have you ever sat around and listened to a bunch of people from Louisiana spin a yarn? If not, you are missing out on one of the greater things in life. Arrange a visit to Louisiana immediately.) We answered all their questions about Aggieland and our unique traditions as we tried to pretend our lips weren't on fire from all the spicy crawfish.

Texas A&M has a great tradition called the Twelfth Man. The students stand for the ENTIRE game to show our willingness to get in the game if needed. It's a beautiful thing, even if it is a bit impractical, because really? What am I going to do if they put me on a field with large men wearing pads, who also want to kill me? However, I gladly stood in the student section for the entirety of every game. But standing on an already wobbly metal bleacher after eating a ton of crawfish and then jumping up and down while cheering for the Aggies? It's a less than desirable combination.

We'll always remember those Ragin' Cajuns fondly. They weren't much on the football field, but man, did they know how to throw a tailgate party.

What I remember most from that day, though, is looking at my group of friends sitting there among those crazy Cajuns as we talked and laughed and tried not to get crawfish on our game-day apparel and feeling such a deep sense of gratitude for those people, that place, and that moment. I knew that for the rest of my life, being with Tiff, Jen, and Gulley would always feel a little bit like coming home. That's how you know your true friends: you hear their laughter and look into their eyes, and it feels like coming home.

CHAPTER 8

The Importance of Showing Up

There is nothing I would not do for those who are really my friends.
I have no notion of loving people by halves; it is not my nature.

JANE AUSTEN

A COUPLE OF months ago, Gulley and I were sitting around with our husbands and talking about college, when we suddenly remembered a night when we were at a place (I'm using the word *place* instead of *bar* because *bar* sounds so tacky and *club* sounds so much cooler than it was, like we were Beyoncé or something) called Hurricane Harry's, and Gulley decided she wanted to sit for a while. So she put her bottom on the edge of a barstool to hoist herself up, only to come to the startling realization that she had actually hoisted herself into a trash can. And so there she was, with arms and legs askew, hanging out of what had to be a very filthy trash can. Being the good friend that I am, I immediately offered her assistance.

Or at least that's what I meant to do, but I was laughing so hard I couldn't stand up and tears were running down my face. It was a good three to four minutes before I gained enough composure to help her out of the can.

As we finished telling our husbands this story, while wiping tears from our eyes, they looked at each other and then asked, "Why are y'all so dumb?"

Sadly, they aren't the first people to ask this.

The rest of junior year flew by. We filled our days with going to class and meeting for lunch, and our weekends were all about Aggie football games until spring came, when we switched to baseball games. Gulley and I continued to be inseparable, but Tiff was becoming more and more serious about the new boy she was dating, and Jen always felt the need to actually study for classes. So while we didn't necessarily drift apart, we spent less time together as a foursome than we had the year before.

We made plans to all share a house the following year, but Tiff announced late that spring that she wasn't going to come back to school in the fall. Her boyfriend was leaving to go play minor league baseball, and she wanted to live at home in Wichita with her family instead. And we understood her decision, even though we hated to see her go.

The four of us had seen each other through broken hearts, family drama, academic crises, and more road trips than I can even remember. We'd laughed together, cried together, and when things got really tough, baked cookies together. We'd been on diets that involved eating jalapeños, limiting our sugar to only marshmallows, and drinking eight glasses of water a day. We'd shared inside jokes, clothes, secrets, and everything in between. We'd become our own version of a family the way you do during college, when you live with your friends and can't pretend that they haven't seen every part of your soul.

And even though we knew it couldn't go on forever the way it was, I don't think any of us were ready for it to end so soon. Sometimes the end of an era comes when you still can't comprehend what that time meant—how it shaped you, and how you'll still miss it sometimes, even twenty-five years later.

So after Tiff let us know she wasn't coming back for her senior year, Jen, Gulley, and I decided we'd find a place for just the three of us to share. The only problem was that we'd waited too long to find a decent place to live in the crowded College Station housing market and ended up in the tiniest duplex you've ever seen—and it was about fifteen minutes from campus. We also soon discovered that the duplex came complete with a stray cat, which we adopted as our own and named Mr. Wendal, after the song of the same name by Arrested Development, since he was our very own bum.

Mr. Wendal has freedom
A free that you and I think is dumb
Free to be without the worries of a quick to diss society
For Mr. Wendal's a bum

It's safe to say I spent the better part of my college career living on the wild side. If you'd asked me, I would have said that I was a Christian, but that was in the same vein as you might say, "I'm one-quarter German." It was an interesting historical tidbit about me, but it didn't affect my life in any significant way.

I guarantee I didn't miss too many Thursday nights (or Wednesdays, Fridays, or Saturdays for that matter) at my favorite hangouts, as opposed to all the mornings I didn't actually make it to class. For me, class was just something I had to do on occasion so I could get decent grades and my dad would continue to pay for the whole thing.

I'm sure that when he reads this, it will make him feel proud of that investment.

In fact, Gulley and I took golf as our PE class one semester and failed. The F was not due to our lack of golf prowess, although it could have been, but because we skipped class eighteen times. We obviously had more important things to do, like work on our tans. Plus, the golf teacher had once been Gulley's Sunday school teacher, and she assured me there was no way he would fail us.

She was wrong.

Gulley and I lived on what I like to call a "convenience-store diet" throughout most of college. We would stop at 7-Eleven on the way to class in the morning and start our day with a Big Gulp. Dr Pepper for her, real Coke for me. Most days, we each bought a package of powdered donuts to go with our sixty-four-ounce beverages. After all, breakfast is the most important meal of the day, and we weren't savages.

On Tuesday and Thursday mornings we'd head to our intercultural communication class and daintily sip our carbonated drinks and eat our powdered donuts while we listened to Professor Gonzales lecture about, you know, culture and communication. Or at least I thought I was listening until he handed back our first exam and I discovered I'd made a 13.

A 13.

As he was about to pass out the graded tests, he gave a brief lecture about how most people did pretty well with the exception of one person who had made a 13. Gulley laughed and wrote a note on my paper that said, "Maybe it was you. Ha. Ha."

It was me.

Ha. Ha.

After I got that test back, I gathered up my donuts and industrial-sized beverage and headed straight to my academic adviser's office to let her know I would be dropping the class. I mean, let's be honest, I might not know much about intercultural communications, but I was well aware that you can't recover from a 13.

Usually after a hard morning of academic achievement, Gulley and I would stop by 7-Eleven again for another Big Gulp, because everyone needs a little afternoon pick-me-up, and what says pick-me-up better than 128 ounces of caffeine and sugar?

Reflecting back on this time, I have a few thoughts:

1. Did I drink even a sip of water during my college career?
2. Why could I not figure out that maybe part of what was contributing to my ever-increasing weight was the fact that I was easily consuming two thousand calories a day in beverages alone?
3. Do college students still drink Big Gulps, or have they become extinct with the advent of Starbucks?

It's interesting that these days, unless I'm on a road trip, it would never even occur to me to drive to a convenience store for the sole purpose of purchasing something to drink. Sonic, yes. Quik Mart, no.

During that year we always stopped at the same convenience

store—the one right around the corner from where we lived. Obviously, we were frequent customers with our average of four to five visits a day. We even knew all the cashiers.

One night Gulley's mom called and asked her, "Do you know somebody named Al?"

Gulley thought about it and said, "No, I don't think so."

Her mom said, "Well, someone named Al called here looking for you and said he knows you from the Quik Mart."

Oh the shame.

We quickly realized that Al was one of the cashiers at our favorite stop. It seems he had gotten Gulley's phone number from one of her checks and called to ask her out on a date. And Al wasn't exactly date material for a variety of reasons. First and foremost because he was at least thirty-five years old, which of course was ancient. Fortunately, the number on her check was her parents' home phone number, not ours.

Gulley and I talked about this story a few years ago, and I remarked that it was kind of scary that Al got her phone number from her check.

Gulley replied, "I'm not sure what's scarier—that he got my number from my check or that I wrote a check for ninety-four cents to pay for a Big Gulp."

These days we are much more sensible and would never write a check for ninety-four cents. We'd use a debit card.

The best part is that twenty years later, Gulley ran into a convenience store on the other side of town while we were visiting her parents, and you'll never believe who was working behind the counter. That's right. Al. And he recognized her, after all these years. Which means two things: Al has an amazing memory, and we should all be using the same wrinkle cream that Gulley uses.

Meanwhile, we saw less and less of Jen even though we all lived in the same 750 square feet. Most days I only saw her briefly early in the morning, when she'd walk into the room Gulley and I shared to wake us up before she left for her eight o'clock class. I'd continually point out that we didn't have class until ten thirty, but she'd inform us that it was good for us to be up early. She also constantly turned the thermostat up and told Gulley and me that the reason we needed to keep it so cold was because we had a higher percentage of body fat than she did. The fact that we loved her in spite of this is a testament to what a wonderful person she can be when she isn't telling people what time they need to wake up or what their appropriate BMI is.

But Jen was focused. She had plans to actually graduate on time the following year and go straight to law school. The only part of this equation that Gulley and I were envious of was the fact that all the cute fraternity boys wanted to be in study groups with her because she was so smart and took the best notes.

Most nights, Jen didn't get home until well after Gulley and I were either settled in for the evening in our pajamas or already out somewhere that wasn't the library. One night there was a thunderstorm that caused our power to go out, so Gulley and I lit some candles, sat on the couch, and got into a deep discussion about how thankful we were for our friendship and all that we'd been through together in the last two years. Just about the time we literally began to sing "Wind beneath My Wings," Jen walked in the front door to find us sitting there in the candlelight singing our hearts out.

"What are y'all doing?"

We explained that the power was out, and she let out a big exhale. "I'm so relieved! I thought y'all were just sitting here in the candlelight together and singing for no reason."

Which made us all laugh until we cried, and before we knew it, we'd convinced Jen to join us on the couch and sing along with us, "Did you ever know that you're my hero? You're everything I wish I could beeeeee!" That is, until our neighbors who shared the other side of our duplex began to bang loudly on the adjoining wall, which we took as a sign that they didn't feel we had the musical stylings of Bette Midler.

It was only a few short weeks later that Jen got the call from her grandmother that her dad was dying. This wasn't a surprise, because he'd been suffering from complications of severe diabetes for a long time, but I don't know that you're ever ready to hear that the end is near. She immediately packed her bags and headed home to be with her family, promising to call us as soon as there was any news.

The call we were dreading came just a day later. Her dad was gone, but in typical Jen fashion, she laughed through her tears and told us she'd get back to us with the funeral details. Gulley and I hung up the phone and burst into tears. We hurt because we knew Jen was hurting, but we didn't know what we were supposed to do or what would help her the most. At that point in our lives, neither of us had experienced the death of a loved one.

So we did the only thing we knew to do. We got in the car and drove to Dallas to be at the funeral with Jen. As she and her family walked down the center aisle behind her dad's casket, she smiled at us despite the big tears that were rolling down her cheeks. And that's when I learned one of the most important lessons I've ever learned about what it means to be a good friend: you show up for your people. You don't wait for your friend to ask you to come; you get in your car and go. You don't have to know the right words to say, you don't have to offer sage wisdom about loss and love; you just show up. You hold her hand and hug her neck and wipe her tears. You let her know that you hurt because she is in pain, and you'd do anything to take it from her if you could. You listen while she laughs at the good memories and wishes for more time—for a dad who could see her graduate with her 4.0 grade point average and go on to be every bit the woman he knew she would become.

Of all the things I learned that year, that's what stands above the rest. You show up for your friends, in the good times and the bad times.

And, also, don't put your home phone number on your checks.

CHAPTER 9

All That Glitters Is Not Gold

A true friend knows your weaknesses but shows you your strengths;
feels your fears but fortifies your faith; sees your anxieties but frees your
spirit; recognizes your disabilities but emphasizes your possibilities.

WILLIAM ARTHUR WARD

THE DEATH OF Jen's dad wasn't the only hard thing we'd face that year. I guess the older you get, the more you begin to struggle with real-life adult problems that are significantly trickier to figure out than problems like needing to find an outfit to wear to the Beta crush party on Thursday night.

The summer before that year began (I like to refer to it as my first senior year of college), I went back to Beaumont for a big family reunion. I felt it would be worth the trip because there would be long tables laden with massive amounts of Italian food and a good chance that my great-uncle Paul would clear the dance floor so he could dance solo to "Don't Mess with My Toot Toot." Uncle Paul actually became somewhat of a legend back in the '80s when he performed his "Toot Toot" routine on top of the home dugout at every Golden Gators baseball game, and he was always happy to share his gift of dance with his family.

I remember feeling very grown up and sophisticated as I got ready to attend the reunion. This would be my first family function as a real adult. I mean, I was twenty-one, and I could even drink a beer from the keg, assuming it wasn't floated by the time I arrived. And because I have an odd gift for remembering exactly what I was wearing at any pivotal moment in my life, I can sadly admit that I wore black shorts and a black blazer with shiny gold buttons. With black cowboy boots. I couldn't be more embarrassed.

The reunion was enjoyable—my cheeks got pinched, my neck got hugged, and I ate more than my share of various pasta dishes. Then as the night was winding down, someone had to call an ambulance for my great-aunt Laura. We were worried she was having a heart attack, but as it turned out, she had just overexerted herself on the dance floor.

No doubt she was trying to upstage Uncle Paul.

So as the old saying goes, once the ambulance shows up, the party is over. The family began to disperse, and I called my old high school friend Becky to come pick me up. We ended up at an establishment called the Handlebar. Oh sure, the name may sound classy, but it was just your basic bar.

When we arrived, I immediately noticed a guy I'd had a crush on throughout most of high school. He was a senior when I was a sophomore, and I thought he was dreamy. Becky and I sat at a table and kept glancing over to where he sat with a few friends. Part of me wanted to talk to him, but I was afraid that he wouldn't remember who I was, and this was a point in my life when I wasn't nearly brave enough to risk humiliation. Eventually, though, I caught his eye, and he made his way over to our table.

Not only did he know exactly who I was, but he said he'd thought about me a lot over the years and wondered what had happened to me. Maybe that last part wasn't true, but I fell for the entire thing. And really, why wouldn't he have thought about me? Other than the fact that the last time he saw me I was a lowly sophomore with a real knack for matching her eye shadow to her socks who had adored him from afar?

We talked for the next few hours, and through the haze of beer and smoke, I felt myself totally falling for him. I found out he'd graduated from college and had an actual job. He was a REAL ADULT. An adult with an OCCUPATION.

Finally it was time for the staff at the Handlebar to throw out everyone who was drunk from either alcohol or, like me, infatuation. Real-adult guy and I traded phone numbers and said we'd keep in touch. I drove back to College Station the next day, wondering if I'd hear from him and hoping that I would.

When I walked in the door after class on Monday, there were a dozen red roses waiting for me on the kitchen table with a card from him that read, "Loved seeing you the other night! Hope to see you again soon."

And here's a crucial detail to this whole story. About six months earlier, my heart had been crushed when Boy B (whom I mentioned in an earlier chapter) broke up with me. I was devastated. The kind of devastated that made me not want to get out of bed in the morning and, on the days I did make it out of bed, caused me to call Gulley from a campus pay phone and beg her to pick me up because I couldn't stop crying. And people were staring. Maybe even pointing.

(Yes, I was probably being overly dramatic about the whole thing. What's your point? Some people can sing or dance. I just happen to have a flair for theatrics.)

I'd spent the time since then trying to recover and convince myself that it was for the best. But I didn't really believe it. At that time in my life, I had yet to embrace being a girl who stood on her own two feet and didn't need a boyfriend to make her feel complete. And it didn't help that Tiff had recently come to visit us and showed off her brand-new engagement ring while asking all of us to be bridesmaids in her wedding. I felt like what Tiff had was all I'd ever wanted, and I didn't yet have the wisdom to realize you can't create a lifetime of happiness with just anyone who looks good on paper.

(Even all these years later, it's hard for me to think about the person I was then. I wish an older version of me had shown up to slap some sense into me and say, "Sister, you have the rest of your life to be married. Put a smile on your face, because these are the carefree days that are as fleeting as dust in the sunlight.")

But that day when the roses showed up, I saw it as some kind of sign that life was about to get better. That boy arrived in town the very next weekend and continued to sweep me away into some kind of fantasy world. He was so different from the other boys I'd dated because he seemed like an actual grown-up. It felt like he could offer me the security I'd been searching for. I mean, after all, I couldn't graduate from college without an engagement ring; it would totally go against my life plan. Plus, it would mean that I'd have to think about finding an occupation of my own that would probably need to be something more substantial than teaching swimming lessons to toddlers at the neighborhood pool.

Feminists everywhere are weeping right now. It stands to reason that I never fully understood the old saying about how a woman needs a man like a fish needs a bicycle.

We dated for the next few months, and the subject of marriage came up frequently. When I look back, I'm ashamed to admit that I don't know if I ever loved him or if I just loved what I thought life could be like with him. I think the thing about growing up with divorced parents is that you're always looking for that sense of a complete family. I saw him as a way to make my own family, even though this idea was based more on episodes of *The Cosby Show* than on any sort of reality.

Five months after we started dating, he asked me to marry him and presented me with a breathtaking diamond solitaire ring. If it had been a marquise-cut diamond with some ugly baguettes, I might have been able to say no, but I was powerless against the classic, brilliant-cut solitaire. That stone hypnotized me into believing everything would be okay, even though a voice inside me, which I chose to ignore, was whispering, "Don't do it."

The next few months were filled with plans for our wedding. I was caught up in trying on wedding dresses, guided by the early '90s belief that the puffier the sleeves, the happier the marriage, with bonus happiness points for excessive beading on the bodice.

As an engagement present, his parents offered to send us to a marriage conference. We both came from Christian homes, but nothing in our relationship was based on Christ. I'd spent the past six years running far and fast from everything I'd been raised to believe, and although I had moments when I could put on my Christian exterior for the crowd, I wasn't regularly looking to God for any sort of guidance.

But something happened at that marriage conference. I sat in the various sessions, desperately wanting to ignore everything that was being said, because I knew without a doubt that if I married him, there was no way we'd have the kind of marriage these speakers were talking about. Something inside me began to hurt, and for the first time, I started thinking about what marriage would be like instead of how fabulous I was going to look in my beaded wedding dress that made Princess Diana's appear understated.

On the drive home, we talked about how I was feeling and agreed that we would try to make our relationship more focused on God. Our resolve lasted about twenty-four hours. We were two people who were completely ill equipped to keep ourselves focused on Christ, much less to encourage someone else to do the same. It was the spiritually blind leading the spiritually blind.

Our relationship began to fall apart. It became clear that we were incompatible and together for all the wrong reasons. It wasn't so much that we wanted to be together as that we didn't want to be alone. I spent most nights crying into my pillow because I knew what I had to do but was terrified to do it. What about my security? What about the house we were planning to build with the brick I had so carefully chosen from the three options the builder offered?

When this relationship first began, Gulley had been so excited for me. But I think she knew long before I did that I wasn't as happy as I was pretending to be, because isn't it always easier to see something clearly from the outside than when you're right in the middle of it? I forged a tough exterior in an attempt to hide all the cracks that were beginning to multiply under the surface, and I wasn't about to let anyone, not even Gulley and Jen, see what was really going on.

But the thing about living piled on top of one another in a small duplex is that it's hard to keep anything hidden for long.

There were only so many nights that I could disappear with the phone into the closet and whisper angry, tear-filled words as I fought with my fiancé. Gulley tried to talk to me about it, but I shut her out. I wasn't ready to admit that my relationship wasn't working, and I tried to convince myself that it would all be okay if I just tried hard enough.

But then there came a night when he showed up unexpectedly at our house. He was increasingly jealous and suspicious of everything I did, and he wanted to check up on me. We got into a screaming match, and he punched the wall right next to me, shattering the drywall. He immediately apologized for losing his temper, and I let it go because I just wanted it to be okay.

However, there is no hiding broken drywall from your roommates, who also have their money tied up in the security deposit for the rental property. When I tearfully confessed to Gulley what had happened, she looked at me with tears in her eyes and said, "If you don't break this off, I'm afraid that one day it's going to be more than just a broken wall."

I'd like to say that I listened thoughtfully and carefully to her words, but I just became more defensive until a few days later, when the truth of her words began to set in. Gulley saw this incident for what it really was and wasn't afraid to speak up. She knew it might make me mad, but she loved me as a person more than she loved our friendship in that moment. She risked it all to say what she knew I needed to hear, even if I didn't want to hear it, and I will love her forever for it. Gulley rescued me when I couldn't save myself, and she didn't care what it might cost.

Several weeks later, I finally worked up the courage to break off the engagement, but he promised that things would be different and suggested we see a counselor. There were red flags waving everywhere, signaling "TROUBLE AHEAD," but I decided to give it another try. Even so, I found myself looking for excuses to avoid him or finding reasons why he couldn't come to town for a visit. This type of behavior isn't usually a harbinger of happy times ahead. *I know we're going to spend the rest of our lives together, but I don't really want to eat dinner with you.*

I flew out of town the following weekend for my sister's high school graduation and couldn't wait to get back to College Station on Sunday evening. The spring semester had just ended, but the Aggies were hosting a baseball tournament, and I was looking forward to some carefree days at Olsen Field with my friends. I'd told my fiancé that I was going to be too busy to have him around, but he showed up that evening anyway. When I opened my door and saw him standing there, I wanted to collapse in a heap. I was frustrated, confused, and scared. I felt trapped.

I told him that I had to work the game and that I'd see him when I got back. As I drove to the baseball field in my Honda CR-X, hot tears rolled down my face until I began to sob as if my life depended on it. I don't know if I've ever felt so lost.

Pulling my car into an empty parking lot, I threw up a desperate prayer to the God I'd been ignoring for so long: "God, if you will show me how to get out of this, I will turn back to you. I am a wreck. HELP ME."

Here's what I now know about God that I didn't know then: he specializes in our honest desperation. He doesn't need flowery words or a lot of artificial sentiment, and he doesn't require us to use phrases like "before your throne" before he'll show up. We might as well be real with him, because he sees it all anyway. As much as we can fool everyone around us, we will never surprise God with the honest emotions of our hearts. That's when his grace comes in like an unexpected breath of fresh air, giving us the strength to do what we need to do just when we feel like we're about to drown.

After the baseball game was over, my fiancé and I drove to Luby's to grab something to eat, because nothing says HEALTHY RELATIONSHIP like going out for a LuAnn platter. On our way there, we began to argue about something inconsequential, but by the time we were pushing our trays through the line and deciding between fried okra and mac and cheese, the fight had escalated into proportions that were beyond human reason.

Because God has a sense of humor, it was at that exact moment that we ran into Gulley's grandparents. Of course, we thought we were eating lunch since it was only two thirty in the afternoon, but they were there for dinner. Nena and Granddaddy had never met my fiancé, and they invited us to sit with them. Over the next twenty minutes, they proceeded to tell him how truly wonderful I was and how blessed he was to have found me. It couldn't have been more awkward if someone's dentures had fallen out on the table. Actually, the denture scenario might have been preferable.

We resumed our argument as soon as we got into the car. And by the time we were back at my house, we were barely speaking. I felt like I was going to be sick, but I kept thinking about my desperate prayer hours earlier, letting it run through my mind over and over again. The silence was thick until I finally said, "I can't be myself around you. I feel like I'm constantly walking on eggshells."

He looked at me for a long moment and said, "If that's how you feel, then give me back the ring."

In that moment, grace came rushing in, and I was free from the mess I'd created. He immediately changed his mind and tried to take back his words, but I wasn't going back. I handed him the ring and told him he needed to leave. I didn't watch him pull out of the driveway, but I heard his car start up and then turn down the street as I sunk to the floor in the living room. My tears were a prayer of gratitude for the God who heard me.

After a few minutes I picked myself up and called the main number at Olsen Field, where I knew Gulley was still working a baseball game. I had her paged over the intercom system because that was the only way to get in touch with her. It's this type of scenario for which cell phones were invented, because "Paging Amy Gulley, paging Amy Gulley: your best friend is having a nervous breakdown" isn't really something a crowd of baseball fans cares to hear in the fifth inning.

Gulley was breathless as she got on the phone and heard me crying. "What's wrong? What happened? Where are you?"

I told her I'd given back the ring, and all she said was, "I'm coming to get you."

She made it to our house in record time and found me sitting on the couch staring into space as I tried to wrap my mind around everything that had just happened. She hugged me as I cried with relief and sadness and other emotions I couldn't identify. All the tension that had built between us over the last few months disappeared as if it had never existed, and there were no rounds of "I told you so"—just love.

As I calmed down, it dawned on me how fast she'd gotten to the house, and I asked, "Was the game over?"

"Nope, it was the fifth inning," she said. "But I told them I had an emergency and left." Then she smiled and said, "We're winning by three runs. If we win this game, the Aggies are going to the College World Series. Want to take a road trip?"

My original plan for the summer was to take a full course load so I could graduate in August, since I was supposed to get married that October. But all of a sudden, summer school didn't seem so important. Once my dad heard the full story of all that had transpired over the last twenty-four hours, he agreed to let me go to the College World Series in Omaha in lieu of the first semester of summer school. Truthfully, I think he was so relieved that I'd decided not to go through with this wedding that he would have agreed to just about anything, as evidenced by the fact that he essentially signed on to pay for another full year of college tuition.

Gulley's stepdad took on the arduous task of driving six boisterous college girls all the way from College Station, Texas, to Omaha, Nebraska—a drive that takes eight hours in the best-case scenario and significantly longer with six women in the car. God bless him. I wonder if even now, more than twenty years later, his eye starts to twitch when he hears the sound of anything that sounds remotely like girls singing along loudly and off-key to a Janet Jackson song.

We finally arrived at the Red Lion Hotel in Omaha around two o'clock on a Sunday morning and began to unload our not-insignificant amount of luggage and cart it up to our various hotel rooms. I was laughing at something as I carried my suitcase onto the elevator and heard a voice say, "I love the sound of a giggling girl."

You can imagine my surprise when I turned around to see who'd said it and saw Steven Tyler from Aerosmith standing behind me in the elevator. He was wearing purple-velvet, zebra-stripe pants, and I hate to inform you that I didn't have the presence of mind to launch into a chorus of "Love in an Elevator." It's one of my life's deepest regrets. Never again will I be presented with that kind of opportunity.

But Steven Tyler's enthusiasm at being in an elevator full of young twentysomething girls was quickly quenched when Gulley's stepdad, whom we call Big, walked in right after us and assumed the role of bodyguard. Or possibly potential assassin.

We spent the next week at Rosenblatt Stadium watching the best teams in college baseball. Between games we visited various tourist destinations like the zoo and made our way to the main strip in Omaha, which was basically like being at a carnival full of college students and baseball fans. There was instant camaraderie and lots of singing "American Pie" at the top of our lungs. Of course, this was back before I knew to heed the wise advice of Mindy Kaling: "I don't care if Don freakin' McLean shows up in a red-white-and-blue tuxedo, no one is allowed to sing 'American Pie.'"

Here's where I should mention that Gulley's dad wasn't on board with our road trip to Omaha. He felt like she needed to go to summer school as she'd originally planned, because school was more important than baseball. However, this wasn't a viewpoint we shared. Which is why her dad turned on ESPN one night to watch the Aggies play in the World Series only to see Gulley appear on his television screen, sitting on the bench outside the dugout at Rosenblatt Stadium, blowing a huge bubble while waving at the camera.

I learned several things during the week I spent in Omaha. I will list them for you in case you want to jot them down.

1. There is not one single public restroom anywhere between Wichita, Kansas, and Omaha, Nebraska. If you

find yourself in need of facilities, your option will be a cornfield. Ask me how I know. Or don't.

2. There is a limit to the number of times you can listen to "Whoomp! (There It Is)" without wearing yourself out on it forever.

3. Steven Tyler wears jeans that are smaller than the Luv-Its with the embroidered ice-cream cone on the pocket that I wore in fourth grade. I'd put him at eighty-five pounds, tops.

4. If you have the chance to visit the Henry Doorly Zoo, I highly recommend the polar bears. However, don't feel like you have to wear a leopard-print top with your denim shorts. Sometimes it's better not to theme-dress unless you're going to a fraternity party. I can show you a picture as evidence to further illustrate this point.

5. When you have a broken heart and aren't sure where you're headed next in life, there is nothing like a road trip in a van full of girls to make you feel better about things.

6. If your dad has forbidden you to go on a trip to the College World Series, it's a good idea to stay away from television cameras.

The Aggies were eliminated from the tournament before the championship game, so we loaded up in the van and began the long trip back to College Station. And that's when reality started to set in for me as I thought about the mess I had to clean up when I got home. There were wedding plans to cancel and deposits to get back from florists and caterers. . . . Then a huge complication occurred to me. I looked at Gulley, who was sitting next to me in the back of the van, and began to cry. "I don't have anywhere to live next year."

Since I'd planned to graduate that August, Gulley and Jen had both made other living arrangements, and I hadn't planned for anything other than a wedding.

Gulley looked at me, put her hand on mine, and said, "Yes, you do. We're sharing a room. You're moving in with me."

Because that's what friends do. They speak the truth when you've lost your way, pick you up and brush you off, tell you that you're going to make it to the other side, and cheer you on until you get there.

And sometimes that looks a lot like offering to let you cram a twin bed into a tiny room that wasn't really meant for two people to share.

CHAPTER 10

Whatever You've Done, Whatever You've Become

"It does not seem that I can trust anyone," said Frodo.
Sam looked at him unhappily. "It all depends on what you want," put in
Merry. "You can trust us to stick with you through thick and thin—to the
bitter end. And you can trust us to keep any secret of yours—closer than you
keep it yourself. But you cannot trust us to let you face trouble alone, and go
off without a word. We are your friends, Frodo."

J. R. R. TOLKIEN

IN THE DAYS that followed our return home from Omaha, Gulley and I both ended up needing each other more than we could have imagined. She'd been dating someone seriously for the last several months, but he broke up with her at the end of June, shortly after we returned home from the College World Series. Gulley hadn't seen it coming, and it broke her heart.

In fact, we now refer to that summer as "that time we slept a lot." It was just the two of us in the duplex because Jen had returned home to Dallas for the summer. We agreed to store her bed while she was gone, which was how we ended up with living-room furniture that consisted of a twin bed and a large couch.

Every afternoon when Gulley and I returned home from class, one of us would curl up on the twin bed and the other on the couch, and we'd sleep for hours at a time. I believe this is more commonly known as depression. We were essentially playing possum with our lives. Instead of facing our fears and heartaches, we just slept our way through much of it.

Of course, I don't regret that time we spent sleeping. You always hear people lament that we spend one-third of our lives sleeping, and frankly, I don't see the problem. Sleep is delightful, and had I known how fleeting a good night's sleep would be once I was in my forties, I might have devoted even more time to it in my twenties. I've also heard that the average person spends 115 days of his or her life laughing, and Gulley and I have laughed at least that much together in the twenty-five years we've been friends. So maybe we're just above average in several life categories because we focus on what's really important.

We always woke up in time to go out every night, though, because that was our specialty. And I think we both believed that if we could just keep ourselves busy, we'd be able to block out everything else that was going on. But sometimes the quiet had a chance to sneak in, and one or the other of us would break down in tears. We relied on each other so much in those months, and I think that's when we began to realize one of the truths that has become almost a motto of our friendship: depending on the day, we are each other's mother, sister, friend, cheerleader, or therapist. And let's just say those were some days when we saved each other thousands of dollars in therapy sessions.

All throughout that summer, I would occasionally hear this small, quiet voice reminding me of the desperate prayer I'd cried out in that parking lot and the promise I'd made to God to turn my life back over to him if he'd just rescue me from the mess I'd made. It wasn't so much that I didn't want to make good on my promise as it was that I didn't know how. I felt so broken and beyond redemption. At that point in my life, I'd totally missed the fact that grace and forgiveness are cornerstones of Christianity, and I saw God more as a disapproving, disappointed father who was waiting to punish me—or worse, send me off to a foreign mission field in some place where I'd have to live in a hut with no air-conditioning or nearby mall. So it seemed easier to just continue to live my life, say the occasional prayer, and figure that God really wasn't interested in doing anything with a mess like me anyway.

We made it to the end of that summer, and then it was time to move out of our duplex and into a new house with our friends Meredith and Paige. They were actually friends Gulley had made during the previous year while I'd been busy making wedding plans, and they found out in June that I was going to be their roommate whether they wanted me or not. Fortunately, they welcomed me with open arms.

I need to explain that Gulley is always the one who makes new friends for us. She's an extrovert who can talk to a wall and figure out where it's from and who its grandmother is and what mutual friends they might have from a summer camp she went to fifteen years earlier. This system works for us because I am bad at small talk and just prefer to become friends with whomever Gulley has prescreened and deemed "our type of girl."

Jen had decided to live with two other girls named Jennifer, because they were all equally conscientious about studying and attending class and realized they weren't just in school to attend

Aggie football games, as Gulley and I sometimes believed. We still loved each other dearly and saw each other on a regular basis, but it was time for a new housing configuration.

Gulley's dad showed up to help us move out of the duplex and into our new place, and that's when we learned that he possesses the unique skill of moving someone completely out of a residence in twenty-three minutes. You've never seen someone move with such efficiency and determination. He grabbed every single thing hanging in my closet, dropped it onto a bed sheet that was spread out on the middle of the floor, rolled it up like a giant tortilla, and loaded it into the car. We applauded his catlike speed and reflexes, and he explained that this was a skill he'd developed because he'd helped more than one friend leave his wife while the wife was at the grocery store. Bless it. All I know is that we were grateful to be the beneficiaries of his moving prowess.

I began my second and final senior year of college while sharing a tiny room with Gulley in a house with Meredith and Paige, who quickly became friends as well. It helped that I had plenty of time to get to know them since I was only taking twelve hours that semester, which was significantly more than the four hours I would take that spring (consisting of one class and a lab). I spent more hours on campus meeting various friends for lunch in the Memorial Student Center than I actually spent in a classroom.

But that fall, Gulley, Jen, and I were busy getting ready for Tiff's wedding. We missed her so much and couldn't wait to stand, along with her sisters, as her bridesmaids. She chose dresses for us that were vintage 1993: black-chiffon, two-piece dresses with a top that buttoned with rhinestones down the front and white chiffon sleeves that were so enormous they interfered with our peripheral vision. We decided that all these dresses needed to really complete the look was the perfect updo. So I booked us hair appointments at a really nice salon near my dad's house in Houston, and we went there the morning of the wedding to have our hair styled.

We were not emotionally prepared for the results. Instead of elegant, sophisticated coiffures, we all had something on our heads that resembled what we referred to as "pieces of Chihuahua poop." The stylist had twisted small sections of our hair into little coils that led into what was supposed to be a French twist, and then she shellacked the whole thing into place with enough hairspray to kill a horse.

As we drove to the church to finish getting ready, we strategized about various ways to salvage our respective hair pride and ultimately managed to comb out most of the decorative coils and pin them into the best French twist we could.

But other than our hair, the wedding was beautiful. Tiff was a radiant, glowing bride, and we were thrilled to see her marry Jason. We'd been a part of their relationship from the day he first saw her walk across the baseball field and declared she was the girl he was going to marry. They were our real-life fairy tale and confirmed our belief that maybe there is such thing as a happily-ever-after when you find the right guy.

As we said good-bye to Tiff after the reception, we all fought back some tears knowing that it would be a while before we'd see her again. Jason was playing baseball in the minor leagues, and his career was going to take them far away from us for the foreseeable future. We knew we'd write and call and keep in touch, but watching Tiff and knowing she was now someone's wife made us feel like we were entering into a whole new stage of life. She was a grown-up now, and I think we all knew that our time was coming to enter the real world in our own ways. I was going to have to graduate that spring whether I liked it or not, Jen had plans to go to law school, and Gulley would have just one semester left before she had to figure out things for the future. Time passes, and change is inevitable, whether you're ready or not.

And I wasn't ready. I was still floundering as I tried to get my life together and falling back into so many of my old patterns. I'd started dating another guy who wasn't good for me, and I couldn't figure out why things weren't working. If the definition of insanity is doing the same things over and over but expecting a different result, then it's safe to say I was insane.

Life was starting to wear me down. I was tired, confused, and lonely, and I walked around feeling empty most of the time, even though I had plenty of friends and the occasional class to keep me occupied. Not to mention that I was terrified about the future, because most companies aren't really lining up to hire the girl who graduated while on scholastic probation, and because I obviously hadn't met the right boy to marry and solve all my problems.

Right after spring break, I showed up at Jen's apartment and confessed all of this to her. I knew she'd spent the last year finding her way back to Christ and turning her life around, mainly because Jen isn't quiet about anything, ever, and certainly not something she feels can benefit those she loves. She told me I needed to go with her to a Bible study called Breakaway. And it is a sign of how desperate I felt that I actually agreed to go.

I walked into First Baptist Church College Station that night with low expectations. I'd grown up in church and had been really involved in my youth group once upon a time. I knew all the "right" Christian answers, but I'd fallen so far away that I felt like I was too far gone. God couldn't possibly want me now.

We sat toward the back of the sanctuary, and I remember two

things as vividly as if they happened yesterday. The first was that the minute the worship leader began to sing, I began to cry. Like, ugly cry. The second thing was that a young guy named Gregg Matte walked onstage and began to talk about how we are called to be children of God and to shine like stars in the universe. (That happens to be in Philippians 2, by the way.) But more than that, he talked about grace and mercy and how God loves us more than we could ever imagine. I don't know that it was the first time I'd really heard about God's grace and love, but it was without a doubt the first time I really grabbed hold of it and decided not to let go. It was the beginning of something real for me.

Over the next few months I became friends with a bunch of people who were actively involved with Breakaway. They were unlike any group of people I'd ever known. They talked openly about their faith and made decisions based on what they felt God was calling them to do. I loved spending time with them because, without even realizing it, they were challenging me to be the person God intended me to be and to quit settling for less. They showed me that being a Christian didn't mean I had to spend all my time in prayer meetings and playing miniature golf like I'd done in high school youth group, which was very important to me, because do you want to die of boredom? Go play a round of miniature golf.

By watching these people live their lives, I learned what it means to seek God's will. I'd heard people talk about it, but I'd never seen it in action. Especially not with people my age.

And ultimately, they pointed me closer to not only Jesus but also to my dear husband, who likes to hang antelopes in our living room. But that's a story that's already been told in an earlier book.

It was also during this time that I picked up Max Lucado's

book *No Wonder They Call Him the Savior* and began to read it. His account of the Prodigal Son rocked everything I'd convinced myself to be true about how God felt about me. I had never before understood how much God loved me, how much he wanted me, and how his grace completely covered every mistake I had made. There's a line in that book that sticks with me even to this day, about how God looks at us and says, "Whatever you have done, whatever you have become, it doesn't matter. Please come home."

So I came home.

And God, in return, lavished me with a scandalous amount of grace as he not only filled my life with wonderful new friends who encouraged me and loved me but also brought Gulley right along with me as she began to develop a real relationship with God too. We fumbled our way through this journey together as we encouraged each other, prayed for each other, and found ourselves standing on solid ground for the first time in a long time. Maybe for the first time ever.

CHAPTER 11

An Ode to Citronella, Why I Don't Camp, and the End of an Era

If ever there is tomorrow when we're not together . . . there is something you must always remember. You are braver than you believe, stronger than you seem, and smarter than you think. But the most important thing is, even if we're apart . . . I'll always be with you.

A. A. MILNE

I HAVE SO many happy memories from the rest of that spring. I loved the new people I was hanging out with and how they were able to make the simplest things fun. Up until that point, the majority of my college experience had been about going out and drinking to have a good time, and I was surprised to discover how fun it was to do things like climb onto someone's roof and just look at the stars or get a group of people together for a midnight bike ride around campus or shave someone's head to look like Ivan Drago in *Rocky IV.*

It was right around that time when one of the coaches at A&M asked me if I'd babysit her three-year-old daughter for a week while she and her husband attended a conference out of state. I asked if Gulley could stay with me at their house for the week to provide reinforcement, and they agreed that this was a good idea. Which led many people in our lives to ask who exactly was baby-sitting whom in this scenario.

Gulley and I thought it would be a grand adventure to live in a house for a week and be responsible for a toddler who loved nothing more than dressing up in princess dresses and making us take turns being the evil stepmother. We were also in charge of a brand-new bulldog puppy named Itchy. Here's something you may not know about bulldog puppies. Their back legs are prone to dislocation if you don't handle them properly. This translated into one of us having to be on constant "Itchy watch" to make sure he didn't try to step down into the backyard from the porch step. We had to gently lift him in and out of the backyard. This was as easy as you are imagining for two college girls with the attention span of a cat on Sudafed.

Our main job, however, was to get our little charge up in the morning after a long night of binge-watching *The Little Mermaid*, feed her breakfast, and drop her off at preschool. We envisioned driving through Shipley Do-Nuts each morning, because what three-year-old doesn't prefer a donut for breakfast? For that matter, what twenty-one-year-old doesn't prefer it? You can imagine our dismay when she announced on the first morning, "I don't like donuts. I like eggs. Over easy."

What is this? Denny's?

I informed her that my egg-cooking skills included only the scrambled version, and the wrinkle of her nose clearly communicated that she realized she was dealing with amateurs. Gulley would get her dressed while I scrambled an egg and made some toast, because let's not even pretend like bacon was going to happen. After breakfast I'd commence the arduous task of trying to give her some sort of hairstyle for the day, Gulley would pack her school bag, and we'd drop her off at her preschool and drive straight back to our house to take a nap because we were exhausted from all the demands of caring for a small person. What seemed like such an easy way to make some money had turned out to be one of the hardest weeks of our lives thus far. We were two fools in charge of a child, a home, and a bulldog puppy with a precarious hip situation. It was more than we'd bargained for.

Of course the irony is that twenty-five years later, I'd refer to this whole scenario as your average Tuesday.

And I have to tell you that what really added insult to injury was that when we picked the little girl up each afternoon, her teachers had always completely redone her hair. It sent a clear message that they knew we had no idea what we were doing.

It was a week that almost killed us, but it probably helped us realize that maybe being in charge of a home and a child wasn't something either of us should rush into. But it also felt good to be doing something outside the normal selfish tendencies we had demonstrated so often during those years. The good news is that we kept the child, the bulldog, and ourselves alive for five whole days and set off the smoke alarm only once. Or twice.

One of the people I became the closest to during that spring was my friend Hite (pronounced like *height*). I'd met him a year or so earlier when I interviewed for a student government committee, and our paths had crossed occasionally since then, but I really got to know him that spring as I became more involved with

Breakaway. He took me in and became like a big brother to me, even though we are the same age. And not only did he encourage me in my faith, but he also taught me how to use e-mail.

It's true. I didn't know how to use e-mail in 1994.

Also, I didn't know what a fax was.

Technological trends aren't really my area of giftedness. Which is probably why earlier this week when Apple announced their fancy new watch, my first thought was to wonder who wants to look at their wrists to know what time it is when they could just look at their phones.

Anyway, the one class I was taking that last semester was a poetry class, and the professor announced at the beginning of the term that he wanted us to e-mail him all our homework assignments. This was great except that the entirety of my technological expertise involved typing my college papers on the Brother word processor I borrowed from Jen any time I needed it. As in, I'd call her and say, "Hey, Jen! What's your brother doing tonight?"

In my head I knew that e-mailing homework would involve a computer, but I stuck my head in the sand like an ostrich about the whole thing, until one day when the professor called me to the front after class and explained that I was going to fail if I didn't get my homework turned in. Even I knew by this time that my dad wasn't going to pay for yet another semester of college, so I called on Hite to take me to the computer lab in the Blocker Building to explain e-mail to me.

He patiently showed me how to use the e-mail account I'd been given, type Professor.Smith@tamu.edu in the address line, and add my homework as an attachment. I followed his instructions but announced with all the authority in the world, "This is so dumb! This e-mail thing is never going to take off as a real form of communication, because these addresses are too long and it's all too complicated!"

Bless my heart.

Two weeks before graduation, about twenty of us—including Hite, Gulley, and Jen—decided it would be fun to go camping at Bryan Utilities Lake as kind of a farewell party for everyone who was leaving for the real world. Everyone met out at the lake, and as people began setting up camp, it became painfully obvious that we could be divided into two groups:

Group 1: serious campers who'd spent actual time in an
    REI store
Group 2: novices who believed that camping meant a
    hotel room with a window unit instead of central air-
    conditioning

I'm sure you can guess which group Gulley, Jen, Hite, and I fell into.

The serious campers set up their deluxe tents with their air mattresses and backpacks full of provisions and first-aid kits, while Gulley, Hite, Jen, and I pulled our pillows, a bag of marshmallows, and a fan out of the car, and we were truly shocked to discover there was no electrical outlet in which to plug the fan. Here's the bottom line: Jen packed satin pajamas.

In spite of our lack of preparedness, we had a great time. Everyone cooked hot dogs, sang songs, and told stories. I couldn't remember when I'd had so much fun and declared camping to be a delightful experience. Until it was time to go to bed.

One of the serious campers took pity on our novice contingent and loaned us a blue tarp to sleep on, so we put our pillows down and looked forward to a night sleeping under the stars. Which was great in theory, except that we'd forgotten one key factor about being out at a lake in Texas during May.

Mosquitoes.

I will never in my lifetime forget lying under the stars and trying to ignore the mosquitoes buzzing in my ear, while Hite whispered incessantly that they were "eating us alive." We had literally become a feast for the mosquitoes, and it felt like only a matter of time before they just picked us up and carted us off somewhere with their little mosquito wings. Finally we found a citronella candle and all huddled around it, feeling like it was our only hope for survival and praying the scent would make the torture stop. Hite even composed a poem on the spot, which he called "An Ode to Citronella." I believe he used the word *swella* in it somewhere, because it's hard to find words that rhyme with citronella.

Then at about three o'clock in the morning, the mosquitoes suddenly disappeared like they'd been called home for dinner. We weren't sure what had happened until in their place came thirty-mile-an-hour north winds and pouring rain. That's right: a cold front hit. In May. In College Station, Texas. What are the odds? We might as well have been living in the Old Testament. It was only a matter of time before the frogs and locusts showed up.

We immediately wrapped ourselves up in the sad, little tarp, huddling around the citronella candle for warmth and completely hysterical over our bad luck. We laughed until we cried about our miserable circumstances, which has a way of making a bad situation become one you know you'll always remember. Why it didn't occur to us to get in the car and leave, I'll never know.

What I do know is that in the midst of all that misery, I was with people I loved dearly, and it will go down as one of my favorite nights ever. It was such a gift to be with those people in that place—plagues and all—right before we were all about to go our separate ways.

It was shortly after we returned from our camping trip that Jen talked me into attending a small prayer group that met at the apartment of some guy named Perry Shankle. If you look at my name on the cover of this book, you'll realize this turned out to be a significant encounter, even though it would be more than a year later before I'd realize to what extent.

(You can read more about this in *The Antelope in the Living Room*. Please run, don't walk, to your local bookstore to pick up a copy today!)

Over the next several weeks, the group met at Perry's apartment a few more times, and it was decided that there should be an end-of-the-year celebration involving fajitas. I am never one to turn down guacamole or any sort of grilled meat, so I made plans to attend. Everyone was told to drop off some meat the day before the party so Perry could marinate it or whatever it is you do to meat. I just know I was impressed that he owned a grill.

Jen and I made a trip to the nearest grocery store to buy some chicken for our contribution to the fajita cookout, but when we tried to deliver it, Perry wasn't home. It was May in Texas, which means it was approximately HOT degrees, so we made the natural decision to leave the chicken on his doorstep in the hope that he'd be home soon. We didn't want to wait around for him to get home because we needed to pick up some Diet Cokes from Sonic and hit the pool to work on our tans, and I think it's obvious that our priorities were more important than worrying about what would happen to raw chicken in the sun.

As Perry tells it, he returned home about two hours later to some fresh bacterial nightmare waiting on his doorstep. He immediately threw it away and couldn't believe anyone was dumb enough to leave raw chicken outside in the heat. I know all too well now that there is not much that is dearer to Perry than the use of proper safety precautions at all times. I can only imagine the horror he would have felt had he known that the person who was so unconcerned about poisoning an entire party with salmonella would eventually be his wife.

The most important part of this story is that Jen and I both made huge strides toward the perfect tan to set off our caps and gowns for our imminent graduation from college.

Just a few days later, Gulley helped me as I struggled to get my graduation cap to fit properly on my head and lamented that the torrential rain was going to ruin my hair before I walked across the stage. She and Hite assured me my hair was "holding up beautifully" in spite of the weather and then hugged me tight before I walked off to get to my place in the line of graduates. Jen, true to form, had graduated summa cum laude from the school of engineering the day before, and now it was my turn to get the diploma that I wish I could say I had worked really hard for but truthfully had earned by the skin of my teeth.

I walked across the stage, relieved that I'd made it but sad that it was all over. As I packed up the last of my things in the room Gulley and I had shared over the last year, I don't know that I even comprehended that we would never live together again. At the time, I don't think I could have handled knowing that, but I also had no way of knowing how much our lives would continue to be intertwined.

We drove over to say good-bye to Jen before I left town, and the three of us hugged one another and cried until there weren't any tears left. Sometimes the end of an era hits you so hard that it knocks the breath out of you. That's how this moment felt. We all knew we would always be friends, and we were ready for all the adventures that lay ahead, but we were sad to say good-bye to everything that had been.

Those five years at Texas A&M gave me so much more than the education or even the husband I had hoped to find during my time there. I'd found something deeper than what I always thought I wanted, because God knew what I really needed: friends who carved out a permanent place in my heart. And those friends ultimately helped me find my way back to the God I'd left behind all those years before. He knit my heart together with the people he knew would hold my hands as I walked the path of the Prodigal Son.

Each of them brought out something in me that I couldn't have found alone and taught me what it means to be a friend who shows up, wipes tears, laughs hysterically, cooks a meal, and eats raw cookie dough right out of the bowl. They taught me that friends share their clothes, their hearts, their dreams, and their study notes. Friends give grace, advice, fashion tips, a shoulder to cry on, and some of the best memories a girl could ever want. A real friend will help you push your car across a busy intersection when it stalls, pull you out of a trash can when you fall in, listen to you analyze the same situation over and over again, speak the truth even when it hurts, help you find your way when you're lost, and hold your hand when you have to say a final good-bye to someone you love.

It turned out that my soul mate wasn't just one guy, but I found soul mates with these girls who are some of the greatest loves of my life. There is rarely any other time in your life when you're given the gift of living day in and day out with people who ultimately become your family. If I had grasped that then, I would have cherished it even more and maybe looked into staying in College Station for enough years to earn a doctorate in something. My time in college and these people whom God placed in my life had healed what was broken in me, and it broke my heart to say good-bye to them.

I drove away from Texas A&M with tears falling down my cheeks, in a Honda CR-X packed to the brim, with a better sense of who I was, with a God who was real in my life, and with a bachelor of arts degree in speech communication.

All I needed now was a job.

CHAPTER 12

Let Sleeping Friends Lie

*If you have good friends, no matter how much life
is sucking, they can make you laugh.*

P. C. CAST

REMEMBER THE MOVIE *Reality Bites*? It came out in 1994, the year
I graduated from college, and followed the lives of recent college
graduates living in Houston, Texas. I can tell you that while parts
of it may have been fairly realistic, it made post-college life look a
lot more fun than I found it to be. Mainly because not one time
did my friends and I ever have a dance party to "My Sharona" in a
convenience store. On the plus side, I never had bangs that looked
like Janeane Garofalo's, nor did I ever date a loser with a goatee
that I mistook for sincerity.

The truth is, I packed my car and drove straight to my dad's
house in Houston. I had no job and no job offers, unless you
count the fact that the neighbor across the street wanted me to

teach some neighborhood kids how to swim over the course of the summer. And while I certainly don't mean to brag about all the prestige that comes with that type of job opportunity right out of college, you can see why I can't help but mention it. My liberal arts degree was already paying off in spades.

So my days went from spending time with my friends, driving through Sonic, taking advantage of the ninety-nine-cent menu at Taco Bell, and hanging out by the pool to being awakened by my dad before he left for work every morning so he could ask me what activities I had planned for the day that might result in employment.

"I don't know. Maybe circle these classified ads until *Days of Our Lives* starts at noon and then head over to a pool full of toddler pee around two o'clock to teach some kids how to swim?"

Keep your eye out for my inspirational booklet full of other helpful job search tips that I may or may not be putting together right now using tape and cardboard.

It wasn't long before my dad realized, rightfully so, that I might just decide to live with him and my stepmom forever unless he took this situation by the horns. Thus he declared that, in an attempt to network my way into employment, I had to become a regular attendee at the Aggie alumni breakfasts that were held in a hotel banquet room at the crack of way too early every Wednesday morning. This was basically my worst nightmare. A social function that required me not only to make small talk but to actually approach people and hand them my résumé? And it wasn't like my résumé was very impressive unless you counted my three-month stint as a salesgirl at the Limited Express. Which, hello, those accessories don't just line themselves up on the display rack.

You'd be amazed at how many corporations aren't interested

in hiring someone who graduated with a 2.0 with the bulk of her work experience consisting of lifeguard jobs.

The only thing I had going for me was a very nice leather briefcase my dad had bought me for graduation. I'd fill that thing full of colored file folders and fifty copies of my résumé and walk into those Aggie breakfasts with all the confidence a double-breasted suit from Casual Corner with matching pumps from Payless ShoeSource could buy. Eventually someone took pity on me—or was bowled over by the fact that I'd also worked at Bealls department store during the Christmas holidays of 1990—and offered me a job interview. The only issue was that it involved a job in San Antonio, a city I'd never actually considered calling home.

However, I scheduled the interview because lifeguards can't be choosers, and I was set to make a trip to San Antonio to meet with the sales manager on the last Tuesday of July. Shortly thereafter, I called Gulley, who was in summer school in College Station, and begged her to ride to the interview with me so I wouldn't have to go alone. It takes about three hours to get from Houston to San Antonio, and I knew I'd have to make the trip there and back in one day. I was right when I figured Gulley would jump at the chance for us to take a little road trip together, even though I would be wearing the aforementioned Casual Corner business suit and prepping for my interview by honing my use of words like *therein* and *circumvent* and also the phrase *viable asset*.

Gulley drove to Houston from College Station the night before, and we woke up bright and early on Tuesday morning to make the trip to San Antonio. We made a quick stop for some enormous Diet Cokes, because breakfast. But other than that, it was a fairly subdued trip, given the important task that lay before me when I arrived.

The interview was for a job with a financial company that contracted employees to a local hospital to assist their staff as they invested their retirement benefits, so I was meeting the sales manager for the interview at a hospital located in downtown San Antonio. For some reason, I felt like it might be seen as unprofessional to bring my best friend along for the ride, so Gulley and I agreed that she would just wait for me in the main lobby of the hospital until the interview was over. I figured it would only take about thirty to forty-five minutes tops. I mean, that was allowing at least twice as much time as my job interview took with Limited Express.

What I didn't count on was that the sales manager would interview me for the better part of an hour and then follow that up with a questionnaire I had to fill out so she could better assess my sales skills. I was already worried about how long the whole process was taking as Gulley sat waiting for me in the hospital lobby, when the manager mentioned she'd love to take me to lunch and then to visit the company's main office located on the other side of town. Don't ask me why common sense didn't prevail at that point and I didn't just tell her I had a friend waiting on me, because I don't have a good answer. And the worst part was that I had no way to let Gulley know what was going on.

Finally, as we were driving back to the hospital after lunch and a tour of the offices, the interviewer made a comment about making another stop to meet a girl who would be my coworker, should I get the job. It was at this point that I finally realized I needed to confess that I had a friend who was waiting on me. I still didn't tell her Gulley had driven into town with me, just that I had plans to meet a friend in the lobby of the hospital at a certain time and didn't want to be late. I guess this seemed like a more professional scenario. My thought was that we could walk back into the hospital lobby, I'd see Gulley, and it would appear as if I was meeting a friend who happened to be in San Antonio.

However, as we walked into the hospital lobby, I glanced around to locate Gulley and didn't see her right away. Then finally, on closer inspection, I saw her. Sound asleep. And she wasn't just taking a little catnap; it was a full-on, laid-out, on-a-hospital-waiting-room-couch nap. I think her mouth was even open. She may have been lightly snoring.

Well. This does not look very professional.

The sales manager looked at me as I nervously scanned the room trying to decide what to do at this juncture. "Do you see your friend?" she asked.

I met her eyes and did the only thing I could do in such a precarious situation. "Nope," I said. "I don't see her."

All the while I was praying that Gulley wouldn't wake up from her dead sleep and discover me standing there.

The interviewer offered to wait with me until my friend showed up, but I thanked her profusely for the kind offer while insisting that she go ahead with her day. I breathed a deep sigh of relief as she told me good-bye and went on her way. As soon as she rounded the corner, I shook Gulley to wake her up and basically dragged her out of there as she wiped sleep from her eyes. I was terrified that my entire career would hang in the balance if the sales manager realized that the woman sleeping in the hospital lobby waiting room, who looked very similar to a vagrant who had wandered in from the downtown streets, was in fact my friend.

By the time we got out to the car, we were howling with laughter. The whole thing was just absurd. The long interview, the lobby, the nap, and the fact that I'd just denied knowing my best friend in the whole world. I apologized over and over again for how long everything had taken and that I hadn't been better at figuring out a solution, other than letting Gulley sit in a waiting room for hours, but she gave me grace and said it was one of the best naps she'd had in a long time.

I also found out two days later that I got the job.

I'm not sure that there is a moral to my story except this: when you find a friend who's willing to forgive you after you leave her to sleep for hours in a sketchy hospital in downtown San Antonio, you've found a keeper.

Let's take a moment to reflect on the profundity of that statement.

Quick! Somebody pin that on Pinterest with a flowery border.

CHAPTER 13

I Just Found Out There's Such a Thing as the Real World

Winter, spring, summer, or fall
All you have to do is call
And I'll be there, yes I will
You've got a friend

CAROLE KING

A COUPLE OF months ago we decided to finally update Caroline's bathroom. Our house was built in 1923, and that was the only room we hadn't updated. It was in desperate need of some new plumbing and tile—it's funny how a bathroom really isn't that useful when you can't manage to get more than a trickle of hot water out of the shower. I realize this is truly a first-world problem, but we are first-world people, so let's just go with it. The bathroom needed work. Mainly because I have no desire to share a bathroom with a preteen girl who would try to claim squatter's rights on my makeup bag.

So I began to look at various bathrooms on Pinterest and Houzz that were so luxurious and well-appointed that even my nice, updated master bath began to struggle with self-esteem issues. Caroline and I looked at different options (at one particularly low moment I had to nix her suggestion of a Hawaiian theme with a sunset mural painted on the wall, because NO), and we finally both agreed on this beautiful blue-and-white patterned tile. After some research, I discovered it's made by a small company in California, and I had to contact them directly to get a price quote.

They e-mailed me back with an estimate for the cost of the tile per square foot, and I was thrilled to discover it was very inexpensive. In fact, I was so excited about the price that I decided we should use it to tile the walls and the floor. I had Perry figure out the amount we'd need, because I'm well aware of my mathematical limits, and then I showed him the quote I'd received from the tile company so we could figure out what our total cost would be.

That's when he discovered that the number I'd been looking at while marveling at the inexpensiveness of it all was not, in fact, the cost of the tile per square foot but merely what it was going to cost to have it shipped to our doorstep from California. The actual cost of the tile was significantly more. Like, "more" as in I was about to blow through our entire budget on tile alone. I was quickly demoted from my role as Chief of Bathroom Remodeling.

I tell you this story because it's this lack of attention to any type of numerical detail that should make you feel very afraid that my first job out of college involved helping people invest their retirement money. Here's what you need to know: just because a girl in a very professional Casual Corner business suit appears to know what she's talking about and uses words like *whereas* doesn't mean you should let her tell you about mutual funds.

In late August of 1994, I packed everything I owned into my Honda CR-X and made the drive to San Antonio to start my new life as an adult with an occupation. This would have looked a lot more impressive if I weren't moving in with my aunt and uncle and their four boys, ranging in age from three to sixteen. It wasn't so much like something out of an episode of *Friends* as it was like living in a fraternity house. But they were so kind to take me in, and they shifted the boys around to make room for me to have my own space. And honestly, even though I initially moved in with them to have a chance to save up some money, I was ultimately so grateful for the company, because I had totally underestimated how lonely life was about to become now that college was over.

I spent my days in a small office in a local hospital talking to people about mutual funds and retirement benefits. I didn't even share an office with coworkers, and there was no one to eat lunch with, which is why I spent most of my lunch hours watching a small TV in the breakroom to keep up with the latest on the O. J. Simpson trial. I'd go home every night to my aunt and uncle's house, where my chief companion was my three-year-old cousin, who liked me to watch *Power Rangers* with him. Sure, it sounds glamorous, but he wasn't much of a conversationalist and didn't usually care to hear about my boring day in the world of finance.

I always say now that one of God's best gifts to me was that I didn't get married right after college, because I think I would have believed that marriage was monotonous and boring, while the truth is that sometimes it's just life in the real world that's monotonous and boring. You have to do things like balancing your checking account and buying groceries and be responsible and go to bed right after the ten o'clock news to be ready for your next work day. It's a real snooze.

Gulley had moved home to live with her parents for her last semester of college, and she was just as lonely. I can't even begin to explain how much money we probably spent on long-distance bills over the next six months. I had virtually no social life in San Antonio, unless you count that one date I went on with a guy who wore a pinky ring, and I don't.

We spent every weekend driving back and forth to visit each other, and it's a testament to Gulley that she didn't mind staying with me at my aunt and uncle's house. In fact, they came to expect her every weekend that I didn't make the trek to College Station. And in the midst of all this, I was struggling to figure out how to walk in my still-new relationship with Christ now that I lacked the support system I'd had in college. I visited a few churches but always felt awkward sitting in the pew by myself and longed for that sense of connection I'd found through the Breakaway Bible study. Honestly, I spent a lot of time planning my San Antonio exit strategy until a friend mentioned that I might want to get in touch with Perry Shankle, who had moved back home to San Antonio earlier in the spring. I figured he was better than nothing or the guy with the pinky ring, so I called him to see if he might be interested in meeting me for dinner or something one night.

Perry and I planned to meet for dinner on Halloween night. (I remember this because our waiter was dressed like a waitress from Hooters, and that's the kind of thing that gets burned into your memory whether you want it to or not.) As I was getting ready for dinner and about to walk out the door, Gulley called, and I told her I was on my way to meet a friend. She said, "A friend? You don't have any friends in San Antonio."

I may have lamented about this to her once or twice or fifty-eight times before.

I said, "Remember Perry Shankle, who led that prayer group? I'm going to meet him for dinner."

And she replied, "Oh! Perry Shankle! I can see it now . . . Melanie Shankle!"

I don't know why she said that, because I wasn't even remotely thinking of this as a date (it was more of a social lifesaving device), but how's that for a prophetic word?

Over the next six months, Perry became my closest friend in San Antonio. I eventually found an apartment and moved out on my own. Meanwhile, Gulley graduated and ended up with a job in Austin. We were pretty happy with this, because Austin and San Antonio are just a little more than an hour away from each other, with a large outlet mall conveniently located at the halfway mark between the two cities. There were many nights when we'd meet each other for dinner and shop at the Banana Republic outlet as we worked to expand our corporate-girl wardrobes beyond our Casual Corner suits.

This was in the days of *Friends*, and Monica and Rachel became our spirit animals as we worked to emulate everything from their clothing to Rachel's hair. They made the real world look so much better than what we'd discovered it to actually be as we worked in cubicles and never hung out while exchanging witty banter in a local coffee shop.

By the following spring, Gulley had listened to me analyze my friendship with Perry to the degree that she probably should have earned a doctorate in counseling. At some point in February, I'd realized I had feelings for him that were beyond friendship, and I couldn't tell if he felt the same way.

Finally one night in March, he took me to see *The Phantom of the Opera* at the Majestic Theatre. Now that I've been married to him for seventeen years, I realize he was obviously in love with me because he wore a tie and took me to a musical, but that's the kind of thing you don't know at the time. For all I knew then, he might have just enjoyed the theater. I thought that it might be the night we talked about our relationship, but my hopes were dashed as we sat in the Whataburger drive-thru after the show and he declared, "I haven't kissed a girl in over a year, but you don't really miss it when there isn't a girl in your life that you're interested in kissing."

Well. That was discouraging. It was like he didn't even see how much my hair looked like Rachel's.

As soon as I walked into my apartment that night, I called Gulley and began to cry as I told her what he'd said. Never mind that it was after midnight, and she had to be in her cubicle at State Farm at seven o'clock the next morning. She listened to me and offered some words of wisdom. Specifically: "Don't freak out."

She'd just spent time with Perry and me the weekend before and assured me she could tell by the way he looked at me that he cared more about me than he probably even realized. And sure enough, it was just about a week later when Perry sat on my couch and told me he had feelings for me and thought it might be a good idea if we started officially dating. Sometimes your best friend sees things a lot more clearly than you do.

I hate to use a tired cliché, but the next two years went by in a flash. I know people always say that, but it's the truth. Tiff was traveling around with her husband as he played baseball, Jen had opted out of law school and moved to Chicago to become a consultant for a large firm, Gulley had met the man she would end up marrying and moved to Dallas, and Perry and I became more and more serious.

As a side note, I have to tell you that after Gulley had been dating her future husband for a few months, they went out to dinner, and on the way home, "It's Hard to Be Humble" came on the radio. Gulley turned it up and sang every single word LOUD AND PROUD. When the song was over she looked up and realized Jon was just staring at her. She would learn later that it was at this tender moment he realized she was the girl for him.

He remarked, "I've never known a girl who knows all the words to that song."

And she replied, "Well, you've never dated a girl who grew up with a goldfish named Mac Davis."

We were all so busy living our lives that our friendship became a series of long-distance phone calls, Hallmark greeting cards, and the all-too-rare visits. But we still called one another first whenever the big things of life happened, which was why I called each of them on the evening of April 24, 1997, just a couple of hours after Perry got down on one knee and asked me to marry him.

At that point, I didn't even know when the wedding would be, but I knew who I wanted standing right next to me when I walked down the aisle toward my future: these girls who had saved me from myself, listened as I cried and worried about the future, taught me how to really love a person, prayed for the right man to come along, and encouraged me every step of the way. If there was any group of girls who had the right to wear the navy bridesmaids dresses with the enormous bow in the back that I ended up selecting, it was the three of them.

My wedding was in August, just four months later, and I have to tell you that August is a terrible time to get married if you live in Texas. (If you're single and reading this, I would suggest a nice October or November wedding.) The night before the ceremony, my future mother-in-law hosted a rehearsal dinner at the country club, and as I looked around the room that night, I saw that I was surrounded by everyone I loved the most in the world—my family and my friends who had become family. There was Tiff, pregnant with her first baby and more beautiful than ever; Gulley with her fiancé, Jon, who would become her husband just two months later; and Jen, who took two days off from her busy job just to be with me. I listened as they toasted to my future with Perry and wished me all the happiness in the world, knowing that was what I wished for them as well and realizing that my world would never be dark, no matter what came, because God had given me the gift of their friendship. He'd knit us together all those years ago, and I had no doubt that time and distance would never break our bond.

In 1 Samuel 20:42, Jonathan says to David, "Go in peace! The two of us have vowed friendship in GOD's name, saying, 'GOD will be the bond between me and you, and between my children and your children forever!'" (*The Message*). And that's the key that makes certain friendships deeper than others—when those friendships are formed in God's name. There are those people God brings into our lives and uses as iron sharpening iron to refine us and shape us and help us become more like the person he created us to be.

It happened so subtly that we didn't even realize until years later that God had brought us all together, with all our vast differences, to teach one another how to love him more. This was something we would desperately need now that we were all officially smack-dab in the middle of the real world with husbands, jobs, babies, and all manner of real-life responsibilities.

CHAPTER 14

Wiping Tears and Bottoms

"I don't feel very much like Pooh today," said Pooh.
"There there," said Piglet. "I'll bring you tea and honey until you do."

A. A. MILNE

HERE'S AN INTERESTING fact. My husband, Perry, and Gulley's husband, Jon, grew up together. Not only that, but their dads were fraternity brothers in college. Yet we didn't plan that or even realize it until after Gulley began dating Jon. And then we both got engaged and married within two months of each other. I tend to think this happened because God knew no man would want to deal with the two of us all the time, in addition to the obvious fact that each of these men were what we needed.

The added bonus is that we married men who not only appreciate our friendship but also encourage it. They have come to realize that this saves them from having to analyze a lot of situations they couldn't care less about and gives them the freedom to hunt or fish anytime they want to, since they know we're always happy to have the girl time. This is what you call an all-around win for everyone involved.

For the first year of her marriage, Gulley and Jon lived in Dallas, which was just terrible because it was way too far for regular visits. So we were overjoyed when his company transferred him to Austin, and we could easily go back to our days of meeting at the outlet mall or spending the occasional weekend at each other's houses.

This was in the days before we had kids, and I'm embarrassed to tell you that I used to load up our dog, Scout, and bring him with me when I spent the weekend with Gulley so he could play with her dog, Annie. In all fairness, Scout really did love spending the weekend with Annie, even if it was just because he liked eating the cheap dog food they fed her as opposed to the pricey dog food he got at home. All I know is that he was one gassy dog on the trips back to San Antonio. True confession: in one of our old photo albums, there's even a picture of the two dogs labeled "Best Friends."

As time went on, I guess it was inevitable that we'd start thinking about motherhood and whether or not we were ready to take that next step into the great unknown. Ultimately, Gulley and her husband decided they were ready for a family before Perry and I did, and I was with her the weekend she began to suspect she might be pregnant. I affirmed that her suspicion might be a reality because I'd never seen someone eat a plate of cheese enchiladas so quickly and still be hungry. And sure enough, she called me a week later while Perry and I were on our way home from a beach vacation to announce that she was pregnant.

I was thrilled for her and so excited about the new baby, but I also felt a little scared for what this would mean for our friendship.

God had been so faithful to let us walk such similar paths that this felt like a shift. It felt like maybe I was being left behind, yet I couldn't convince Perry that it was time for us to have a baby by using only the reasoning that Gulley was having one so we should too. That's generally not a great reason to bring a human being into the world. And it wasn't like I didn't have a friend with a baby, since Tiff already had two little girls and another one on the way. But Tiff wasn't as much a part of my daily life as Gulley was, so this felt different.

But as Gulley's pregnancy progressed and I watched her open wrapped packages full of baby blankets and burp cloths at various baby showers, I couldn't help but be excited for what was ahead. A baby. We were going to have a baby.

The low point came when I drove up to visit her a couple of weeks before she was due, and she was so swollen that when she walked in the restaurant where we were meeting, I didn't recognize her. She will tell you herself that she and her husband weighed the same amount by the time she delivered their baby boy, and her husband isn't a small guy.

The weekend before Gulley was due, Jen drove down from Dallas, and we all spent the weekend at Gulley's house, telling old stories and marveling that a baby was on the way and laughing hysterically that Gulley was constantly complaining about how hot she was even though it was the end of January. She was so pregnant that even her tongue was swollen.

In what would prove to be an accurate indicator of his personality, her baby boy didn't show up on his due date. And so two days later, I left San Antonio at the crack of dawn to be at the hospital, where they began to induce labor. Here's what I vividly remember about that day:

1. She didn't want any of the beef jerky her husband offered her while she breathed through a contraction.
2. We were told that if we didn't change the channel on the TV immediately, she was going to get out of bed and throw the entire TV through the hospital window on account of Kelly Ripa's voice.
3. Her epidural didn't really work the way it was supposed to, which sparked some serious misgivings for me about the entire labor and delivery process.
4. The nurses kept insisting that we all needed to go into the waiting room, but I stood right outside the door of Gulley's room with her whole family, and I think they finally realized it was a losing battle. This is also when Gulley's mom offered me a Weight Watchers brownie because I mentioned I was hungry. To this day it might be the worst thing I've ever eaten.
5. When I saw that little, redheaded baby boy for the first time, I loved him like he was my own.

We all got to hold him briefly, but then the nurses whisked him off, so we had to settle for watching him through the nursery window. I quickly declared that he was the best-looking baby of all the babies and that all those other babies looked below average by comparison—never mind that all their relatives were gathered right there by us. I felt like it was clear to everyone that Jackson was the pinkest, healthiest, most beautiful baby ever.

And so Gulley was a mama. To my surprise, this didn't mean that she all of a sudden became a boring person who just wanted to talk about diapers and only wore high-waisted jeans with overly large back pockets.

I had to be in Austin for a business trip when Jackson was about two weeks old, and I skipped out on the company dinner one night so I could go over to Gulley's house to make them a homemade dinner and get my baby fix. Sometimes when people have been bringing you tater tot casserole for two weeks straight, you need your best friend to show up and cook some pecan chicken and homemade mashed potatoes with cream gravy. As I rocked Jackson to sleep that night after we'd eaten dinner, I officially knew that I was going to need to get me one of these babies for myself.

Three months later, I was pregnant. There's a certain security that comes when you see that your best friend is managing to do something you aren't sure you can do, and seeing Gulley transition into motherhood gave me the courage to follow her. Perry and I were thrilled to learn I was pregnant and equally devastated when we found out at a doctor's appointment eight weeks later that there was no heartbeat. We'd lost the baby.

The doctor informed us that we'd need to schedule a D & C, but we'd have to wait for several days because this was the Thursday before Memorial Day weekend. As we left the doctor's office, I began to call everyone to let them know our sad news. I wanted to rip it off like a Band-Aid and get all the pain out at one time instead of having to tell the story over and over again for days.

When I called Gulley, she immediately said she was getting in her car to be with me right then. I assured her I was fine and would let her know when I needed her. All I really wanted to do was climb in bed and stay there for a long time. But God has a way of putting the pieces together when you don't even know what you need, and it turned out that Jen was staying with some friends at a nearby lake house for Memorial Day weekend.

At first I wasn't sure I wanted to be around people, but ultimately I decided it might be good for me to get out of the house. It ended up being good medicine to be around Jen and feel normal for just a little while. But on the way home that night, the reality of the miscarriage sank in again, and the sadness seeped into every part of my heart.

My D & C was scheduled for Tuesday morning, and we were supposed to be at the hospital at six thirty. Gulley called me on Monday night and informed me that she would meet us there and stay until it was over. She didn't wait for me to ask her to come. I didn't even know that I needed her to be there, but she knew.

When Perry and I walked into the hospital waiting room and I saw her sitting there, I began to cry, because that's what friendship looks like: knowing your friend better than she knows herself and being there to hold her hand while her heart breaks.

Because I didn't have kids yet, I didn't even fully appreciate all the details Gulley had to work out to be with me that morning instead of at home with her five-month-old. I just knew I was so grateful.

Over the next few weeks I discovered that I'd had something called a partial molar pregnancy and that it came with some complications beyond your normal miscarriage. I won't bore you with all the medical jargon, but the bottom line is that I had hormone levels that were out of control, so I had to have a series of injections along with regular blood work every week for the next four months as the doctors waited to see if everything was going to be okay. Basically my master plan to immediately try to get pregnant again was thwarted.

And this is where things could have gotten sticky between Gulley and me, because when you're going through one of the hardest trials of your life, and you want something more than anything else in the world and your best friend has that thing, either you can let jealousy and envy creep in or you can ask God to give you strength beyond yourself to not let your hurt get in the way of a relationship. That's what I chose to do, because I didn't want to make the same dumb, selfish choices I'd made in the past.

What grew instead of bitterness was my love for my best friend's precious baby boy, and she recognized that being with him helped heal something in me. So she never failed to let me give him his bottle, rock him to sleep, and spend hours holding him on my chest while I breathed in his intoxicating baby smell.

(Jackson is now almost thirteen and will be horrified by that entire paragraph. I would apologize, but I don't feel one bit sorry for any of it. I loved him then, and I love him now.)

To take my mind off everything that was going on, Gulley and I planned a trip to New York at the end of that October. Jackson was ten months old by then, but she made the arrangements so we could have a girls' getaway to shop and see *LIVE with Regis and Kelly*, which is when we discovered that Kelly Ripa is the smallest person you will ever see in real life. We couldn't get over it.

It was a perfect trip, full of shopping and delicious food and laughter, and on the plane ride home, Gulley discovered she had spent every cent she'd brought on the trip, down to her last dollar, and I was more than happy to give her a dollar so she could purchase some headphones to watch the in-flight movie. The most important thing was that she was leaving New York with a fabulous new leather coat.

A few months later when we attended a baby shower together

for our friend Meredith, Gulley hugged me as I cried on the way home and wondered if a baby was ever going to be a reality for me. She listened as I questioned God's plan and loudly voiced every frustration I'd kept pent up over the past six months. She didn't try to give me nice, pat answers about the sovereignty of God and how he must really trust me to give me such a hard thing. You know what nobody wants to hear when they're really hurting? THAT.

Because the truth is that God often gives us more than we can handle, because he knows we start to believe we can deal with life on our own and our hearts wander further and further from him as we believe we have it all under control. Sometimes the best thing you can do for a person is to listen as they let out all their pain and then let go of the feeling that you need to fix it. Listening with compassion is a highly underrated skill, but that's what Gulley did for me that day—and it's what she has done over and over again throughout the course of our friendship.

When I called her a few weeks later to tell her I was pregnant, I think she was even happier than I was. One of the best things about Gulley is that she gives the best reactions to your news. (Think Kristen Wiig in the surprise party skit from *Saturday Night Live*.) She can barely contain herself. This is just one of many reasons she's always one of the first people I call with any type of life announcement. And she not only gets excited but rates your own enthusiasm and determines if it's appropriate for the situation.

(A couple of years ago I called to tell her that I had a publishing contract for my first book, and she was beside herself. I, however, was cautiously optimistic and tempered my excitement with a lot of statements like "It's going to be a lot of work" and "I'm really overwhelmed" until she finally said, "I NEED YOU TO GET EXCITED, COACH FRAN!" which was a reference to the Aggie football coach at that time, Dennis Franchione, who never showed an ounce of emotion on the sideline, no matter what was going on in the game.)

Over the next few months she was there for every baby shower and there to listen every time I felt nervous about the pregnancy. She offered advice and helped me plan and bought all manner of pink clothing and accessories when we found out I was having a baby girl. (Which may or may not have been before the actual sonogram but rather when she helped me perform the Drano Crystals urine test that Perry declared the dumbest thing he'd ever heard of. I won't claim that it's foolproof, but it did accurately predict I was having a girl.) And when Caroline was born at 2:14 a.m. on Saturday, August 3, Gulley had been waiting with my sister and the rest of my family for hours to meet her.

Some roads we travel in life can feel like the ones that might break us, but that's why God surrounds us with people who will cheer us on and wipe our tears and listen as we pour out our hearts. Because often, it's not what you say but what you do that really matters. Like rocking your best friend's new daughter to sleep when she feels like she's at the end of her rope after three hours of sleep yet feels a little guilty about complaining because she prayed so hard for this moment to happen.

CHAPTER 15

Living Life to the Realest

I would rather walk with a friend in the dark, than alone in the light.

HELEN KELLER

LAST MONDAY MORNING, Caroline woke me up at six o'clock to tell me she'd forgotten to mention she needed a meter board and some plastic tubing for school that day. I was sound asleep, so it took me a few minutes to process this information.

"You need a what? What's a meter board?" I asked groggily.

"Mooom, it's a meter board. You know? A meter board. I need one of those and some plastic tubing." She looked at me like I was dense.

Am I living in an episode of *CSI*? Is David Caruso about to walk in and put on his sunglasses while uttering a ridiculous line? Because why does a sixth-grader need plastic tubing and a meter board?

As it turned out, she needed the supplies for the extracurricular course she had signed up for, because they were building a roller coaster. And I found out that a meter board is a piece of plywood that measures one meter by one meter. Apparently kids today actually use the metric system. I remember being force-fed a lot of Metric Man cartoons back in elementary school, but it didn't stick with me, and you'll never persuade me to measure something using centimeters instead of inches.

So we ended up at Home Depot at 7:15 a.m. You know where you don't want to be at 7:15 a.m. on a Monday? At Home Depot with a surly eleven-year-old. It might make you stop in the middle of the plumbing aisle as you search for plastic tubing and announce, "If your attitude doesn't improve RIGHT THIS MINUTE, I am going to lose my mind, and you're going to lose your phone."

Taking the phone has become the best tool in my parenting arsenal, and I use it liberally. It produces immediate results every time. Feel free to use it at will.

We finally found someone to cut a piece of plywood so it measured one meter by one meter and procured the plastic tubing. The only remaining dilemma was how my tiny girl was going to get the board into school by herself, and we decided the only option was for me to carry it for her. This was obviously a mortifying scenario for her because I am a hideous troll who continually seeks out new ways to embarrass my child. It's like I'd planned an elaborate scenario in which I could carry a meter board into the junior high just for fun.

And so she walked ten feet ahead of me while I carried this board like I'm just a weird lady who likes to haul plywood into educational settings. I'm discovering that being the mother of a junior high kid is humbling.

That's what I told Gulley that morning when she called me on her way to work, and she agreed. Her oldest son, Jackson, is also in junior high, and we agreed it's not for the faint of heart or the insecure. It's a new stage of parenting that is incredibly exhausting mentally, with all manner of absurd scenarios we couldn't have imagined back when we were parenting during the toddler years. Those years were more physically exhausting, and I think Gulley and I survived only because we had each other.

Right before Caroline was born, Gulley's husband, Jon, was offered a new job that meant they'd be moving to San Antonio. You can't even imagine the joy we felt over this development. And then when Caroline was eighteen months old and Gulley's son Jackson was three, Gulley had her younger son, Will. So between the two of us, we had three kids who were each eighteen months apart. I meant to have another one eighteen months after she had Will, but then I got too tired and forgot. What I remember from that time was how many days Gulley and I called each other by eight o'clock in the morning, desperate to make a plan for the day to save our sanity and let our kids burn off some energy. They were like little monkeys but worse, because we didn't have the option to put them in a cage or shoot them with tranquilizer darts. Those years are a haze of dirty diapers, chicken nuggets, epic meltdowns, sand throwing, potty training, sleepless nights, and sticky little hands that could find any pair of white jeans in a six-mile radius. It's a wonder we survived.

The summer when the kids were two, three, and five, it rained almost every day in July, which meant the neighborhood pool wasn't an option, and we were all left despondent and hanging on to our sanity by a fragile thread. One morning Gulley and I planned to take the kids to the free Wednesday movie at a local theater but decided we didn't feel like driving across town in the pouring rain to go see *Clifford's Really Big Movie*, otherwise known as parental torture in the form of a large red canine film with a marginal plot.

So after we ruled out the movie, Gulley asked, "What are we going to do all day in this rain?"

And I said, "Caroline and I are going to pack a sack lunch and spend the entire day at your house."

And that's exactly what we did. Except that we didn't pack a sack lunch, because that's why McDonald's was invented. Some people think McDonald's was invented for the McRib sandwich, but the reality is that it was created for mothers of toddlers who are willing to exchange nutritional value for a decent, albeit germ-infested, playground.

However, I did pack several of my kid-friendly DVDs, including *Muppets from Space*, along with a pair of new jeans to show Gulley so she could try them on and see if she needed a pair for herself. The kids all ran back to the playroom while we attempted to have a conversation and engage in deep analysis over the jeans situation, but we kept getting interrupted because the gang felt they needed to ice-skate in the living room. So because the rain had driven us to desperation, Gulley and I got in her bed, closed the door, turned on the Food Network, and just let the children take over the entire house. We felt like as long as they didn't burn it to the ground, we didn't really care what they did. You want to ice-skate in your socks in the living room? FINE. They had broken us down like we were pack mules.

Every now and then one of the kids would come in and ask us for some juice or something, and we'd say, "Why can't you people leave us alone? Don't you know we're busy discussing the way Giada pronounces *fettuccine Alfredo*? This is serious, serious stuff."

Finally, we realized it was probably time to feed everyone lunch, and we emerged from the safe haven of Gulley's room to discover that the kids had torn the place apart. And we didn't even care. We'd watched Giada make a delicious pasta dish and figured out the jeans situation, and it was worth it. It was totally worth it.

While we debated about what to do for lunch (the age-old dilemma of McDonald's versus hot dogs: delicious and nutritious either way), the kids began playing with a whoopee cushion. I'd like to say that Gulley and I were above it, but we weren't. We gave in to the siren song of the whoopee cushion, and we all took turns seeing who could give the most realistic portrayal of intestinal distress, loudly applauding all the dramatic efforts. This is called a Motherhood Low. It was all fun and games until Jackson got a little too enthusiastic and popped the whoopee cushion. Everyone was pretty upset about it, but Gulley told him to just go get the other one out of the playroom. It was a proud moment for me to realize that my best friend has a two–whoopee cushion home. I mean, anyone can have one whoopee cushion, but to have a spare? That's just dedication to a lost art form.

It was shortly after this point that we decided it would probably do us all good to get out for a little bit, seeing as how we were down to our last whoopee cushion, so we loaded everyone up in the car and drove through the pouring rain to pick up McDonald's Happy Meals. We got home, ate our Happy Meals, and had a little rest time. Gulley and I could have easily reverted back to our college days and taken a four-hour nap, but the kids wouldn't even sit still for a movie. After an hour of repeated demands for Popsicles and Chex Mix, we gave up the dream of nap time and decided to let them bake cookies.

The sad part is that we felt it had been a full day, yet it was only one o'clock in the afternoon. We discussed taking the kids to the museum but decided to show them some real culture instead—to teach them a skill that would serve them well throughout the rest of their lives. We went bowling.

We laced up our bowling shoes, grabbed the lightest bowling balls we could find, and had ourselves a little tournament while Gulley and I sang lyrics from the bowling scene in *Grease 2* that I don't believe were ever actually intended to be about bowling.

A great time was had by everyone except Will, who felt like the world was conspiring against him, because that's how you feel when you are two years old. Sadly, none of us broke one hundred in spite of the bumpers in the gutters, and I felt Gulley should be ashamed of herself because she took bowling for a kinesiology credit at A&M and really didn't play up to her potential.

We headed home, proud that we had turned what could have been a dreary, boring day into a day of fun and adventure. And I'm not even talking about the adventure that comes when you visit a bowling alley in a sketchy area of town, but the fun that comes when you just all enjoy being together and make the most of what could be considered mundane. Because that's what best friends do: they take even the most boring days—days when your child says things like "I'm sadder than a pickle that's been eaten"—and make them better.

That fall, Gulley decided it was time to enroll Will in a preschool program. She knew I adored Caroline's preschool, but she was a little apprehensive about signing him up to attend the same school. Her reason can be summed up in three words: SHOEBOX FIESTA FLOAT.

(Is shoebox one word? If not, her reason can be summed up in four words: SHOE BOX FIESTA FLOAT.)

(If you've read my first book, *Sparkly Green Earrings*, you are fully aware of my skills in this area.)

She had been witness a year earlier to her best friend turning into some sort of lunatic who called various McDonald's restaurants and begged them to hold Happy Meal toys for her. She had seen my dark side. It was kind of like when Obi-Wan Kenobi had proof that Anakin had darkness under the surface. Actually, I don't know if it was like that at all, because I have very limited knowledge of anything related to *Star Wars*. I just wanted to throw that in there. Plus, I'm trying to expand my *Star Wars* horizons, because the other day a little boy asked me some question like "Do you know what the Prince Commander of Blah-Blah-Blah and Rebel Force Blah-Blah-Blah when blah-blah-blah?" I had absolutely no clue what kind of answer he was looking for, so I just answered, "TWO?"

Have you ever had a five-year-old look at you like he pities you? Yes, me, too.

Anyway, because I had some pride issues involving my ability to make shoebox fiesta floats, I promised Gulley that when the day came that Will had to take part in the shoebox float parade, I would help her make the float.

Late that spring, she received a note from school informing her that it was time for the kids to make their floats. She called me up so we could schedule a day to hit Michaels for the necessary supplies and then go back to my house to assemble the whole thing. I'd be lying if I said that I wasn't a little excited to have the chance to use my hot-glue gun. I'm a little embarrassed that I just admitted that, but I do occasionally like to get my craft on.

The good news is that Gulley had the float theme all thought out because I had taught her well. She'd benefited from the error of my ways a few years earlier when I'd desperately searched for all the Happy Meal Wizard of Oz characters, to no avail. Her sister's in-laws had brought her boys the entire Happy Meal collection of *Madagascar* animals over Thanksgiving (with the exception of Gloria, because I have a whole conspiracy theory that McDonald's may be anti-hippo), and she'd been saving them for such a time as this. I had never been more proud to call her my friend.

We met at Starbucks and then headed to Michaels to purchase ribbon, glitter paper, and other various float materials. It never occurred to either one of us that maybe we should purchase some sort of life. And then we went back to my house and began to work on the float, stopping only for lunch and the occasional Diet Coke. At one point it did occur to us that maybe it was a little bizarre that we were spending our entire day working on a float for a three-year-old who would have been just as happy, if not happier, if we'd handed him a shoebox with a whoopee cushion glued to the top and called it a poop-mobile, but then the hot-glue gun began to burn my fingers and I forgot what I was talking about.

By the time Gulley left to pick up Will from school that day, my living room floor was covered in glitter, and we had most of the float finished. I instructed Gulley to go home and let Will glue on the rest of the tissue paper flowers because, after all, it was his float. It's not like we were going to do the WHOLE thing for him.

And sure, some people may say the zebra-print arch with "I like to move it" written on it is a little over the top considering no one in his class could even read, but to those people I say that you've never experienced having your Barbie Island Princess float put to shame by a float that's pulled by an actual battery-operated horse.

We put our hearts, our souls, and the tips of my fingers that were burned by the hot-glue gun into that float, and we couldn't have been more proud. And it served as proof that the two of us can have fun together doing anything. But more important, these years we've spent raising our little people have taught us so much more. We've learned how much you need a friend to share the days with—someone who can reassure you that it's probably normal that your son has an imaginary friend named Mr. Bing, who has a mom with only one boob and lives in Mexico. You need someone safe to talk to about the struggles of nap time and when to make your children get rid of the pacifier and if they're going to end up in long-term therapy because you made them drink a full cup of water and sit on the toilet for thirty minutes until they couldn't help but pee in the toilet instead of their diaper.

And this needs to be someone you can trust with your struggles and tell the real story to, as opposed to what you see posted on Facebook and Instagram, which just give a happy snapshot of life. Social media is fine and good, but it rarely resembles real life. We all need those people in our lives to whom we can show our real selves without fear of judgment or shame. And we need to remember that often the reason some people feel the need to Instagram a perfectly filtered photo of themselves playing a board game with their four-year-old while drinking hot chocolate is because that's the only time they've done that EVER. People love to show off their Disney vacation photos but often neglect to mention that they had to eat ramen noodles for three months to pay for it.

Over the years, Gulley and I have worked on our marriages, our sanity, our homes, our weight, our fashion, and our strategies for getting a toddler to quit throwing a wild-eyed fit. We've been real with each other and admitted our failures, our disappointments, our frustrations, and the fact that we've resorted to Benadryl to get a kid to go to bed. We've cried real tears and laughed until we couldn't breathe and cheered each other on as we've each tried to find our way through the labyrinth they call motherhood.

You know how at some point in life you had a friend you daydreamed with, and you thought how great it would be if you grew up and lived down the street from each other and got to see each other every day and your kids could grow up together and be best friends?

Gulley is that friend for me.

When we met almost twenty-five years ago, I couldn't have imagined that someday we'd live a mile away from each other and that we'd get to live real, day-to-day life together and that our kids would love each other as much as we love each other. But we do. And they do.

CHAPTER 16

Ain't No Party like a Wrapping Party

We are best friends. Always remember that if you fall, I'll
pick you up . . . just as soon as I quit laughing.

AUTHOR UNKNOWN

EVERY YEAR, RIGHT around September, Gulley and I get together for a calendar meeting to plan our annual Christmas Shopping Weekend, complete with the Wrapping Par-tay. (It must be pronounced just like the women used to say it in the Walmart commercial. This is critical.) And yes, I meant to capitalize it because it is an event. For almost as long as we've been friends, we have designated one weekend in early December as an exclusive girls' weekend, when we spend forty-eight hours finishing all our Christmas shopping and then eating a variety of cheeses on Saturday night while we wrap every last present.

Back in our college days, most of this weekend was spent looking for a cute outfit to wear on New Year's Eve and charging it to our dads' Visa cards. Shout-out to the Guess boot shoes of 1992!

But as our lives changed and the bulk of our Christmas shopping became focused on our kids, we began most of these weekends at Toys"R"Us. Rumor has it that's where a kid can be a kid, and while that is all good and fine, it's also a place where mothers have been known to instantaneously double up on their birth control pills. I can't explain how loud and chaotic the store is on a Friday night two weeks before Christmas. There are kids crying and begging in every single aisle. It honestly feels less like a quality shopping experience and more like a hostage situation.

Many times, Gulley and I just end up standing next to our cart and gazing blankly at a huge wall of Star Wars toys while she asks me if I think the DC-17 Skywalker Fighter Jet (probably not its real name, because PLEASE) is better than the Rebel Fighter blah, blah, blah, and I'm all like, "Why are you speaking to me in a foreign language? No comprendo el Star Wars." This is usually about the time when we realize that we are overwhelmed not only by all the kids being kids but also by the fact that Toys"R"Us is clearly charging upwards of five dollars more per toy than Target does.

However, even in Target, things aren't necessarily easier. The prices might be better, but often we still have no clarity about whether the Rebel Forces are the good guys or if a Tinkerbell Styling Head is better than an Island Princess Barbie Styling Head or how some of those little stuffed animal puppies manage to look trampy even though they're just dogs.

There was one year when the only thing I knew was that if Santa didn't show up at my house with a Diamond Castle Barbie horse and carriage, we were going to have sad times. And Target was sold out, which was ironic considering I'd seen that dang carriage every time I'd been at Target for the last two months but refused to buy it early since I didn't know where I'd hide it for the next two months, because guess what, Barbie? Not everyone lives in a castle.

That Saturday, Gulley and I got up bright and early, stopped at Starbucks, and then threw caution to the wind by making our way to Walmart. And this is where I owe Walmart a huge apology, because sometimes I give them a bad rap on account of all the patrons on scooters who block the aisles. Not only did Walmart have the Diamond Castle carriage, but the store was also clean and orderly. No one was more surprised by this turn of events than I was, but I found it to be a delightful shopping experience. In fact, it restored any Christmas cheer I'd lost the day before. The only remaining issue that year was trying to figure out when Ken started wearing V-neck sweaters and carrying a man purse. Don't try to call it a messenger bag—it's a purse, Ken.

Over the years we have looked for every hot toy you can imagine. We've come home and bid for hard-to-find things on eBay, we've walked miles at various malls and shopping centers, we've talked each other down from buying absurd toys in a frantic attempt to make Christmas magical, and we've kept track of Christmas lists that would make Santa Claus seem unorganized. We take this seriously. We are two women on a mission, and we only make occasional stops to refuel with Diet Coke and a sugar cookie. One year we felt like we had time to go to the movies on Friday night, and Gulley ordered both the large popcorn and some M&M's, because as she declared, "I brought my Zantac, and I'm ready to party this weekend." This felt like both a high and a low point for our annual shopping weekend.

After all our shopping is completed on Saturday night, we usually finish at the grocery store to buy all kinds of unhealthy snacks and stuff to make cookie dough that will be eaten straight from the bowl and never baked into actual cookies. Then we stay up into the wee, small hours of the night wrapping presents and tying bows and losing multiple pairs of scissors and rolls of tape as we watch movies and discuss everything from the politics of elementary school to college football to my ongoing dilemma over whether I should have bangs.

I mention this tradition because I highly recommend it for every woman. It takes something that can be frustrating and time consuming and turns it into a fun girls' weekend that you can totally play up to your husband as "working hard to give the family a wonderful Christmas" because you're just that selfless. And if you're like me, you can even offer to buy a few Christmas presents for yourself while you're out. Plus, our kids get so excited to see all those beautifully wrapped presents under the Christmas tree when they get home from wherever their fathers have taken them for the weekend.

Gulley and I realized last year that we didn't really need to go to Toys"R"Us anymore. Our kids are a little bit older and all about the electronics instead of the Star Wars action figures or Barbie dolls. I think it made both of us a little sad, because those little years went by so fast and nobody wants a toy kitchen anymore. But that's the beauty of walking through life with a friend. When you realize that one stage might be ending and another one beginning, she helps you look at the bright side. And the bright side looks a lot like Christmas shopping that basically consists of buying a bunch of iTunes gift cards and having more time to see several movies in one weekend.

Of course, we'll still stay up late on Saturday night to wrap the gift cards anyway because, after all, it's a tradition.

CHAPTER 17

The Road Goes On Forever and the Party Never Ends

On the road again
Like a band of gypsies we go down the highway
We're the best of friends
WILLIE NELSON

SEVERAL YEARS AGO, Gulley and I took the kids to Dallas to stay at the Great Wolf Lodge. Our friend Alissa had won a free stay in an auction and offered to let us use it because she really had no need to experience an indoor water park as a single woman in her late twenties. And truthfully, this may apply to everyone. Maybe it's because I'm a native Texan and there are really only two months each year that aren't fit for outdoor swimming, but all that chlorine and water and people in swimsuits in a huge indoor facility just doesn't seem natural to me. In fact, it seems like a recipe for a stomach bug, which is exactly what Gulley's younger son, Will, caught on our last day there.

The truly unfortunate part was that we needed to leave Dallas and drive to Bryan that day. So we loaded up in the car with plenty of plastic bags, Clorox wipes, and the kind of steely fortitude that would have impressed our pioneer ancestors, and we began the arduous and vomitous three-hour drive to Gulley's mom's house in Bryan. When we reached the halfway point, Will was still letting out a high-pitched scream every time he had to throw up, which was often. That's when Gulley asked from the back of the car where she sat with Will, "Who thought this was a good idea?"

It was a valid question.

Gulley and I have loved road trips ever since all those years ago when we went to TCU with the Diamond Darlings. It doesn't take much for the two of us to decide to pack up the car and hit the open road. We even have a foolproof system: I do the driving no matter whose car we're in, we stop often for snacks, and we make each other laugh until someone spits her Diet Coke across the car.

And so it makes sense that we have passed on our love of the road to our kids. We took them on their first road trip when they were all still in car seats, and we were desperate for anything that seemed remotely like a vacation. We ended up having such a good time that it became an annual tradition. Now we spend every year planning a weeklong summer road trip to various destinations within the state of Texas. Rumor has it we may even be entertaining the idea of venturing out of state now that the kids are older, but we'll have to see if I can get a prescription for some Xanax first.

In our early years of motherhood, we had only one destination: the home of Gulley's mom and stepdad (aka Honey and Big) in Bryan. We would pack up the car until we looked like the Joad family from *The Grapes of Wrath* and then make the three-hour trek with frequent potty stops, since nothing takes control of your life like kids you're desperately attempting to potty train. Gulley is more fun than I am because she came up with the idea to let each kid pick out a bag of candy for the road. Jackson and Will usually chose Skittles, while my child opted for Circus Peanuts. Heaven help me, I have a child who would choose Circus Peanuts over something normal like M&M's or Reese's Peanut Butter Cups. Circus Peanuts are essentially just glorified Styrofoam packing peanuts and, if this is possible, taste worse than those sugared orange slices that everybody's grandparents used to keep in glass candy dishes on the coffee table.

We would arrive in Bryan desperate to find activities for the kids but also just glad to be together, because everyone was always thrilled at the novelty of being out of town in a new place. These were simpler times, even if you include the summer Will developed a predilection for breaking any sunglasses he found in his path. I can't tell you the sadness I felt one morning when he walked in holding two pieces of what used to be my sunglasses as he looked at Gulley and tearfully said, "Mom, I need to tell you about something that wasn't an accident."

And we could always count on Gulley's grandmother Nena to come over and provide us with some entertainment, like the time we all watched *The Bachelor* season finale together. Nena had never experienced anything like this in her entire life, and this is a brief sample of her running commentary: "HONEY, ARE YOU TELLING ME BOTH OF THOSE GIRLS THINK HE'S ABOUT TO PROPOSE? I'VE NEVER HEARD OF SUCH. I CAN'T STAND TO WATCH ANYMORE! WAIT, TELL ME ABOUT THIS CUTE BLONDE. WHAT DOES HER MOTHER THINK OF HER BEING ON THIS SHOW?"

(This was always Nena's standard question. It was imperative for her to know what someone's mother thought about the situation.)

Watching *The Bachelor* led to a discussion about marriage, and Nena told us that she and Granddaddy had NOTHING in common, except, WELL, he really liked to eat, and she likes to eat too. You don't really hear people mention that specific commonality in premarital counseling, but it must have been enough because they were happily married for sixty-six years.

She also informed us she has always gotten her hair cut by only well-known hairdressers who cut famous people's hair. (This isn't exactly true, but she likes to say it because the woman who used to cut her hair once cut Barbara Bush's hair.) Anyway, she'd been debating whether she should let one of the aides at the assisted-living home cut her hair. Gulley and I told her she needed to feel free to say no, because you can't trust just anyone with your hair.

Then there was the visit when we arrived in time for dinner, and Nena surprised Honey by making a vegetable casserole to go along with the meal. I knew all I needed to know when everyone went to serve their plates and no one helped themselves to Nena's casserole. I think we were all scared because when Gulley asked her specifically what kind of vegetables were in her vegetable casserole, she replied, "Vegetables." That's the sort of vague answer that lets you know there's a can of Veg-All somewhere in the mix.

After we all finished dinner, Nena cornered me in the kitchen and said, "Melanie! I want you to taste some of my vegetable casserole while it's still warm!"

And it was at that moment that Gulley, my best friend in the whole world, threw me under the Veg-All bus. She wouldn't even look at me, but I saw her holding in the laughter as she fled the scene. In fact, the whole family fled the scene and just left me there. Alone and defenseless. I picked up a fork, wondering all the while how I could get out of this situation gracefully, especially since I'm finicky about the texture of my food. Water chestnuts have been known to make me dry-heave, so you can only imagine my fear of canned, unidentifiable mixed vegetables.

Just as I was certain my casserole fate was sealed, Caroline yelled out, "Mama! I need you to come help me get in the bathtub!" I was saved by the bath.

The next day I told Nena that her casserole was delicious. In all honesty, I didn't try it, but for all I know it could have been delicious, and I didn't want to hurt her feelings. And then she gave me the recipe, which, as I'd suspected, contained a can of something she referred to as Stokely's Mixed Vegetables. Ew.

These were the years when the kids spent the ride home from every trip declaring that it was "the saddest day" of their entire lives, and they were going to "cry myself to sleep all the way home" because they didn't want to leave. But Gulley and I always knew we wouldn't get that lucky.

Instead they usually opted to take out their sadness in the form of extended whining over the fact that Will was humming a song quietly to himself. And then Will, sensing his power, continued to hum quietly to himself while staring directly at the offended party.

It was usually at this point that I dispensed the first of many pieces of wisdom that would be given throughout the duration of the ride home: "It's all fun and games until all that whining means we don't get to stop for a DQ Blizzard in Bastrop."

This statement usually caused an instant reconciliation in the backseat, and Gulley and I were then free to get caught up in our own in-depth conversation about profound matters like people's tendency to think the grass is greener on the other side, but you know what's over there? MORE GRASS. In fact, *It's Just More Grass* may be the title of the self-help book I'll never actually write. We also liked to discuss our eyebrows, and we came to the realization that no matter how much you pluck or shape them, they will always just be sisters, not twins.

But my personal favorite words of wisdom came from Gulley during the last thirty minutes of the trip, when she broke up a backseat scuffle by declaring, "When you lick the person sitting next to you, there's a good chance you're going to get punched."

I believe the only reason that gem is missing from the book of Proverbs is because Solomon must never have traveled with three kids in the back of his chariot.

Our road trips in the last few years have presented different challenges as the kids have gotten older. We now find ourselves with a car full of tweens who are often surly and lacking in complete development of their frontal lobes, which means they lack basic common sense the majority of the time. Case in point: last summer Caroline kept tooting in the backseat until I finally said, "Caroline! You need to stop! A day is going to come when boys won't think it's attractive or funny for a girl to toot in the backseat!"

And Jackson dryly replied, "Yes. That day is now."

In the weeks leading up to our most recent summer road trip, we debated and analyzed possible destinations and couldn't figure out the best plan of action. But then one night we were eating dinner with a friend who mentioned the Flying L Guest Ranch in Bandera. She said they had a cute water park with a lazy river. We looked it up on the Google and decided it sounded fun. We also noticed they offered horseback riding, but you know what sounds miserable in 106-degree heat? Being on a horse. And everything else.

The drive to Bandera was only about an hour, and when we pulled up to the Flying L Guest Ranch, we saw a wave pool, a giant slide, and a place for Gulley and me to buy drinks and sit in the shade.

It was perfect.

We sunscreened the kids, and then Gulley and I spent the next five hours floating and eating and listening to the classic country music being piped in over the loudspeakers. We sang along to "I Was Country When Country Wasn't Cool," and Gulley reminisced about the Halloween when she dressed up as Barbara Mandrell. Which isn't to be confused with the time she sang "Delta Dawn" in her fifth-grade school program.

Eventually we'd all had enough of the sun and the water, not to mention that Caroline had a blister on her toe that she wouldn't quit talking about, so we got back into the car and began our journey to Austin, where we planned to spend the night.

And here's the observation we made. Our kids don't think we're as smart as they used to think we were. They know A LOT for people who can't even drive. They have A LOT of opinions. And they're LOUD. We spent more than several minutes informing them that we are in charge and that we know how to get places and that we're NOT GOING TO EAT AT APPLEBEE'S in Austin just because they've decided they like chain restaurants with questionable food.

Really, it's Caroline and Jackson who are the worst offenders. But even Will got in on the action later that night while we were watching a sporting event on TV. The announcers introduced one of the competitors, and Will said, "OH, I HATE AUSTRIANS."

What? You hate Austrians?

My first thought was that perhaps he'd had a bad experience with *The Sound of Music*. Because that's really the extent of my knowledge of Austria. And I've never heard anyone express a dislike of Austrians before, so I couldn't really imagine what the problem might be.

Gulley said, "What on earth? Why do you hate Austrians?"

"Well, because their country is filled with snakes and poisonous creatures."

"First of all, I'm pretty sure you're thinking of Australia. And, second of all, it's a great place, and you don't need to hate anyone or anything. Especially when you don't know anything about it," Gulley replied.

"Well, it's also where they send the people from Mexico when they're bad," he countered.

And that's why you don't really need to listen to anyone under the age of ten. Especially on matters of geography or restaurant choices, because then we might all be eating at Applebee's and have unfounded issues with Australia.

And that's really no good for anyone.

We spent the night at a hotel in Austin and the following day at the Bullock Texas State History Museum, which totally exceeded my expectations. And also confirmed that I didn't pay much attention in my seventh-grade Texas history class. I'm sure it was because I had bigger things to worry about than Santa Anna—things like what to wear with my sweet new pinstriped Guess jeans and if my purple eye shadow was the right shade to wear with my new purple polo, because everyone knows your eye makeup and clothes need to match.

But if the goal of the museum is to make people feel an even deeper sense of pride for our state, then it succeeded, because Gulley and I barely made it out without buying T-shirts featuring a large cannon with "Come and Take It" written on the front.

The only low point was when we came upon an exhibit that featured a button you could push that released the smell of sulfur as it came out of the ground, and Jackson decided it was a good idea to push his mother's face into it. See? He's lacking in frontal-lobe development, because who thinks that's a good idea? Although he quickly realized the error in his judgment when Gulley yelled, "WHAT IS THE MATTER WITH YOU? WHAT ARE YOU DOING?"

Ironically, these are the same questions we've yelled since they were toddlers, but now we're just asking them for different reasons.

Occasionally Gulley and I get to take a road trip sans kids, just like in the olden days, except we have to bring Zantac in case we eat too much junk food. This wasn't an issue when we were in college. I'm also right on the brink of needing glasses to see the road signs. In other words, PARTY ON.

About ten years ago, Tiff and her family settled down in College Station after her husband was done playing baseball, and since she lived closer, it was easier to spend time together. By this time, Tiff was expecting her fourth baby, and Gulley and I decided it would be fun to make the trip to surprise her at the hospital. After all, by the time you're having your fourth baby, you wonder if your husband is even going to show up.

In typical Tiff fashion, she'd spent the day and night before her scheduled C-section making the prettiest cookies I've ever seen and wrapping them in clear plastic bags and tying them up with brown ribbon and tulle to hand out to all her nurses and any of her visitors. Seriously.

And I will tell you that the hospital staff was knocking themselves out to take care of her. Even housekeeping got in on the action and was in her room begging for something to clean after they heard the rumor about the new mom with the cookies. In fact, I had to fight some of them off just so I could grab about three or nine for myself. Needless to say, Tiff and her baby were the hit of the hospital, and I decided right then and there that if I ever had another baby, I would bring something real nice, like some beef jerky sticks and perhaps an economy-size bag of chips for the hospital staff to share, because, obviously, it's the little things that count.

We were so glad to see Tiff and meet her darling new baby boy, and we all settled into the hospital room and laughed and talked and reminisced over how dumb we all were and marveled over how God had entrusted us with our husbands, our kids, and our friendship with one another over the years. It was one of those moments when the time seems to melt away, and we realized that the years hadn't done anything to erase how much we all loved one another.

Several months after that, Gulley and I took another sans-kids trip to College Station for a Diamond Darling reunion. Tiff and Jen were going to meet us there, but we purposely got in early on Friday night because we felt it was our duty to explore some Texas A&M landmarks, such as the Dixie Chicken. And this won't mean anything to you if you aren't an Aggie, but Northgate is completely different now. I mean, it has paved parking and parking meters. And even a parking garage. It has come a long way from a couple of mud lots behind the Chicken.

We walked up to the entrance, optimistically hoping we'd have to show our IDs, and the guy working the door looked at us and said, "Y'all are good, I don't need to see ID."

Thank you. Thank you very much. A hint of uncertainty would have been nice.

Once we walked in, we saw that everything was EXACTLY the same. The smell, the smoke, the old guy passed out while sitting upright. It was as if time had stood still.

We walked around just to absorb the ambience, which is exactly what you'd expect from a place called the Dixie Chicken. And we ended up meeting the ESPN crew that was in town to cover the football game. One member of the crew was a girl who had recently graduated from the University of Kentucky, and she asked us when we graduated from A&M. We countered by asking how old she thought we were.

She took a long, deep breath and said, "Please don't be offended, but I'm going to say twenty-seven."

Gulley and I were thrilled until we realized that when you're twenty-two you cannot even conceive of an age as high as thirty-six. I mean, do people even live that long?

And if they do, they certainly don't do anything other than lug their eighteen kids around in a minivan and watch *Murder, She Wrote*.

Around midnight we decided it was probably time for us to head home because we're old, and we walked back to the car. We had parked in one of the new lots and put enough change in the parking meter for an hour. I was worried we were pushing the limits of our hour.

Now, I need to give you a little history about me.

While I was a student at A&M, parking was a mess. It was like survival of the fittest just to find a spot to park every day. And yes, I could have taken the shuttle bus, but if you honestly think I'd take crowded public transportation full of college students with morning breath, then you don't know me very well.

This meant I was always running late, and I usually just had to park wherever I could find a space. Staff parking. Twenty-minute parking. University-president parking. Wherever. Let's just say I may still owe Texas A&M several hundred dollars in parking fines, unless there is some kind of statute of limitations. I had a complicated relationship with UPD, otherwise known as the University Police Department. The UPD was my arch nemesis—well, besides the Whataburger taquitos, which singlehandedly caused me to gain twenty extra pounds my sophomore year.

My point is that due to my constant parking issues with UPD, I am very sensitive to parking tickets and expired meters. So when Gulley and I were walking back to the car and I saw a policeman standing in the vicinity of my vehicle, I immediately lost my mind and raced over there to let him know, "HERE I AM! PLEASE DON'T GIVE ME A TICKET!"

As Gulley and I rounded the corner, we got the full view of the policeman whom I thought was about to give me a ticket, and he was wearing shorty shorts, combat boots, mirrored sunglasses (at midnight), and a badge that declared him to be a "Detective of Love."

I'm not sure if it was the shorty shorts or the badge that gave away the fact that he was not, in fact, UPD but rather a fraternity boy dressed up for Halloween. But I'm pretty sure it was the shorts, because they definitely seemed to lack a professional "I'm a University policeman" vibe.

Although the belt and the water gun were a nice touch.

Needless to say, Gulley and I collapsed into hysterical laughter. I mean doubled-over, can't-breathe laughter. And as soon as we recovered, we asked the guy's girlfriend to take a picture of us with him. As she took the picture, we told them we were former students back for a reunion and the game.

The girl squealed, "OMIGOSH, y'all are SO CUTE. What are y'all? Like twenty-seven?"

I replied, "No, we're thirty-six."

And I'm not exaggerating when I say that she recoiled in horror, mainly because I think she was afraid we'd escaped from the nursing home.

After our run-in with the "police" on Friday night, we went home and slept the sleep of angels. You know, the kind of sleep you get when you know for sure that no one is going to need you to help them go potty in the middle of the night. Then on Saturday morning we headed to Olsen Field to meet Jen and Tiff at the Diamond Darling reunion and alumni baseball game.

We sat in those stands just like we did all those years ago when our friendship was brand new, and it was like no time had passed at all—each of us so familiar to the others that it was like being wrapped in a favorite blanket. Since those early days, we've seen one another through bad breakups, first dates, meeting THE ONE, weddings, miscarriages, babies, deaths, career changes, missions trips, and more crises of the hair than you can imagine. All of it has served to strengthen our ties and make us appreciate what a gift we have been in one another's lives.

We have lived out the encouragement the apostle Paul gave to the Colossians: "Since the day we heard about you, we have not stopped praying for you. We continually ask God to fill you with the knowledge of his will through all the wisdom and understanding that the Spirit gives, so that you may live a life worthy of the Lord and please him in every way: bearing fruit in every good work, growing in the knowledge of God, being strengthened with all power according to his glorious might so that you may have great endurance and patience, and giving joyful thanks to the Father, who has qualified you to share in the inheritance of his holy people in the kingdom of light" (Colossians 1:9-12).

As time passes, it's rare that we're all together at the same time, but it's always soul filling to have a little bit of time together and watch the years fade away, leaving only our comfortable familiarity and easy laughter in their wake.

Here's something else I learned that day: there is only so long you can watch old baseball players play baseball.

Non-exciting doesn't really even begin to cover it.

At the end of the weekend, Gulley and I got in the car to head back home with our hearts full of love and renewed strength to face another week of motherhood and the PTO and dinner making and life in general.

Because maybe that's what a road trip with a friend does most of all: it takes you on a heady mixture of both new adventures and places marked with familiarity and comfort. And the joy of it leaves you grateful for all that is behind and ready to face everything that lies ahead.

CHAPTER 18

Going through the Big C—and I Don't Mean Chocolate

When we honestly ask ourselves which persons in our lives mean the most
to us, we often find that it is those who, instead of giving much advice,
solutions, or cures, have chosen rather to share our pain and touch our wounds
with a gentle and tender hand. The friend who can be silent with us in a
moment of despair or confusion, who can stay with us in an hour of grief and
bereavement, who can tolerate not-knowing, not-curing, not-healing and
face with us the reality of our powerlessness, that is the friend who cares.

HENRI J. M. NOUWEN

LAST SUMMER I was in the dressing room at Everything But Water, experiencing the crime against humanity known as swimsuit shopping. If only I was as motivated to work out during the other 8,759 hours of the year as I am during that one hour each spring when I have to find a swimsuit. I finally put one on that didn't make me want to hurl. It was a lovely shade of turquoise, had a top that was flattering and supportive, and offered two different options for the bottom. Therein lay my dilemma. One was more of a traditional bottom with a ruffle, and the other was more like a fitted swim skirt with ruching. I was a little concerned that both bottom options had the potential to make me look like a hippo about to perform a ballet routine.

I had to make a decision right then and there, because there was only one pair of each bottom left in my size. So I did the only thing that could be done in such a desperate time: I called Gulley to see if I could text her photos of myself in each swimsuit option and get her honest opinion. It wasn't as good as having her there in person, but it would have to do.

I cannot even express how many times I checked and double-checked to make sure she was the only person I was texting those pictures to. Can you even imagine the horror of inadvertently sending a photo of yourself in a swimsuit to the wrong person? I have no idea how many various friends and acquaintances' numbers I have stored in my cell phone, but I can say with all certainty that 99.9 percent of them don't need to receive a picture of me wearing a swimsuit in a fluorescent-lit dressing room. After much back-and-forth texting and deliberation, Gulley helped me decide on the right bottom. In the end, we felt like it was the best choice. No pun intended.

When I got back in my car with my new swimsuit purchase, I thought about how much you have to trust a person to send them a picture of yourself in a swimsuit, with all your flaws laid bare. And I realized it's kind of a metaphor for friendship in general—being willing to let someone see all your weaknesses and knowing they won't broadcast them to the world. Because life has a way of throwing things our way that aren't always pretty, and they can leave us vulnerable, hurting, and in desperate need of someone who will help us carry our burdens until we're safely on the other side.

I realize I just took a big emotional leap from the simple act of trying on a swimsuit, but that's the way my mind works. Welcome. I hope you'll stay awhile.

As the years went by, most of my friends from college got married, had babies, and took on thirty-year mortgages, but Jen remained single. She'd call and tell us about an occasional date, but the right guy never seemed to come along. But what I love about her is that instead of pouting over her singleness and distancing herself from her married friends, Jen always showed up. She wore more than her fair share of ugly bridesmaid dresses, rocked our babies, prayed for us through the ups and downs of marriage, and always invested in our lives. She took missions trips to Africa, taught a Bible study at her church, got a master's degree from Dallas Theological Seminary, bought her own house, and pursued a successful career. Sure, she hoped to get married, but she built a life for herself that wasn't focused on that one goal.

Then a few years ago she brought a guy named Scott to visit for the weekend. They'd been dating for a few months, and things seemed pretty serious. There was talk of marriage, but they eventually broke up. He was a confirmed bachelor and just didn't know if he was ready to make a commitment, and things fell apart. Jen was heartbroken, and we were heartbroken for her, but we trusted that God must have something else for her life.

About a year and a half later, I received a text message from Jen that read, "Scott and I just got engaged!"

Um. I'm sorry, but I'm confused.

So I texted back, "Did I miss something? I didn't even know y'all were dating again."

(Because, listen. If anyone is going to miss some kind of major detail, it's me.)

But I hadn't missed anything.

Scott and Jen had spent eighteen months apart, but he never quit thinking about her. Ultimately, he decided that he didn't want to spend his life without Jen. So he went to her mom and asked for permission to marry her, bought an engagement ring, and then showed up and told Jen they needed to talk. He declared that he knew she was the girl for him, placed the ring on the dashboard of the car, and said he was ready to put it on her finger the moment she was ready.

And in typical Jen fashion, she began screaming, "I'M READY! I'M READY!"

IT'S LIKE A SCENE RIGHT OUT OF A MOVIE.

So he got down on one knee, placed the ring on her finger, and they were married three months later. It was a day filled with love and close friends and family, tears, laughter, and so much joy. A day we'd all hoped would come.

Since Jen's dad had passed away many years before, she walked down the aisle alone. As she got to the halfway point, Scott left the front of the church, went to meet her, and walked her the rest of the way. And everyone broke into applause. It was one of my favorite wedding moments ever. Watching one of your dearest friends live out her fairy tale has to be one of the sweetest gifts life offers.

So it was almost more than we could stand when Jen called Gulley and me just a few months later to announce that she was pregnant. This news was much like her engagement in that it came as a bit of a shock since the last thing she'd told us about her and Scott's plans for a family was that they were going to take at least a year to wait and see. She was thirty-nine, and he was forty-six, and they just weren't sure if kids were going to be a part of their lives. But you know what they say: we make our plans, and God laughs because he has something else in store for us that's beyond our wildest imaginations. This wasn't a planned pregnancy by any stretch, but it was an example of how God knows us better than we know ourselves.

It was just a couple of months after her one-year wedding anniversary that she and Scott welcomed their new baby boy into the world. We were all overcome with joy as we watched Jen become a mom. And we were amazed at how easily she adjusted to the whole thing after all those years of being able to walk out her front door without worrying about packing a bag full of diapers, bottles, and wipes—and also remembering to grab the baby, which is always crucial to the whole leaving-the-house thing.

Maybe it was because she'd watched so many of her friends struggle to figure out motherhood that she adapted to it so well—she'd had a front-row seat to what really mattered and what didn't. I never saw her stress over all those things first-time moms tend to agonize over: there was no scouring every surface with antibacterial wipes, or insisting the baby needed to stay on his schedule or life would be ruined. She even drove all the way to San Antonio with him when he was just a few months old to help celebrate my fortieth birthday, and she had him dressed in a homemade onesie she'd painted herself that read, "I love Aunt Mel. Fabulous and forty and soon to be famous." At least the forty part was true. But see how much she loves me?

As we all sat around that weekend watching Aggie football, eating cookie dough, and holding Jen's new baby boy, the whole thing just felt like a miracle. But what we didn't know then was that the real miracle was still up ahead in the distance.

※

One day a few months later, I drove out to Nordstrom to meet my friend Leah for coffee. I didn't even realize that Nordstrom has a coffee shop that opens before the store does, because I lead a sheltered life and rarely venture beyond my neighborhood Starbucks. But Leah suggested Nordstrom, so I threw caution to the wind and drove outside my normal bubble to meet her.

And the Nordstrom coffee was delicious. I was kind of worried it would disappoint because I'm so used to Starbucks, but it was a nice change. And I say that like I'm a real coffee connoisseur, but I assure you that in reality a fancy restaurant could replace their normal coffee with Folgers, and I'd be hard pressed (I so want to say *French pressed* right there) to know the difference.

Anyway, as I was making the long, twenty-minute journey to see Leah, I decided to call my friend Jamie and say hi, because she is really the reason why I know Leah. (And I should also tell you that I met Jamie in college through Jen, because they were best friends in high school.) But since Jamie lives in Dallas, she couldn't meet us for coffee, and I wanted her to know she would be missed.

On a side note that has nothing to do with anything, Jamie and I call each other Evelyn. Or sometimes just Ev for short. This started more than ten years ago when she lived here in town, and we'd get together and trade magazines every week. Gulley said we were like two little old ladies with our obsessive magazine swapping, so we began to call each other Evelyn. This was back in the days before Pinterest made home-decor magazines practically irrelevant.

Evelyn and I did a quick catch-up on life, and then she mentioned that she and her husband were taking a trip with their boys over spring break. She made the comment that it was a good time to do it since they were all healthy, and you never know what the future holds. And honestly? I thought it was kind of a depressing thought. It wasn't that I didn't agree with her, but I just don't spend a lot of time thinking about those things. I prefer a little strategy I call denial.

At that point in our conversation, I arrived at Nordstrom, so we promised to talk soon and hung up. Then Leah and I spent the next two hours laughing over coffee and having a lengthy discussion about what types of jeans are appropriate for forty-year-old men, because we have reached a point in life where we are married to forty-year-old men.

I spent the rest of the afternoon shopping until it was time to pick up Caroline from school. Caroline and I made our way home, and I was going through her backpack, looking for notes and soggy graham crackers left over from the snack I'd packed that morning (because she is fundamentally opposed to actually putting the remains of her snack back into a Ziploc baggie), when I heard my phone ring and then immediately beep with a text coming through. It was Jamie, and she said to call her as soon as I could. Which I thought was weird because we'd just talked earlier.

So I called her back. And that's when she told me that she'd just talked to Jen, and that Jen had found out that afternoon that she had breast cancer. She'd asked Jamie to call her close friends to let them know.

Jen.

Jen, who had been there for me more times than I could count, who made me laugh until my stomach hurt, who had been a part of my heart for more than half of my life. Jen, who had gotten married just a little less than two years ago and was mom to the most darling eight-month-old boy. Jen, who had always eaten healthier than anyone I knew and who exercised and did all the right things—all the things we're told to do to give us the illusion that we can control whether or not we get cancer.

After I hung up with Jamie, I called Jen. We talked for just a little bit, and she was good. Upbeat and optimistic, talking about the pink scarves she planned to wear after she lost her hair, because "pink is my signature color." Her prognosis looked good, but we both knew enough to know she was at mile marker one of what was going to be a long stretch of road.

And then I hung up the phone and cried. Then I called Gulley, and we cried together. Because there's a hurt that hits so deep that it takes your breath away and leaves nothing but tears in its place. It's hard when one of your people has a tough road ahead.

I spent the next few weeks crying at times that caught me by surprise, like in the drive-thru line at the bank when a certain song came on or at the grocery store when I noticed that candy conversation hearts were on sale and remembered they're Jen's favorite. I didn't want her to be at the doctor's office having tests. I didn't want her life to involve surgery and chemo and a million insurance documents. I wanted her to be lying on a blanket in the sunshine next to her baby boy, blowing bubbles and listening to him laugh.

I realize that people get bad news every day. And I realize all of us have all kinds of difficult things on our plates. But there are times it hits really close to home, and this was one of those times for me.

But the thing is, God had surrounded Jen with the most amazing community before she ever received a cancer diagnosis. People went out of their way to help her however they could because she'd spent years doing the same thing for them. She has a heart that loves God and trusts him to a point that never fails to humble me. This is what she said in an e-mail just a few days after she knew she was facing surgery, chemo, and radiation: "Our God's gone before us in so many very visible ways to remind us that though it's a shock to us, it's NOT a surprise to him! He's paved the way in precious and gracious ways. He knew this was coming in 2012, and he surprised me with Scott in 2010, and then he surprised us with Linc in 2011. So the surprise of cancer is so graciously buffered by those other surprise gifts of grace. My heart is overwhelmed with gratitude. And he has granted a peace that surpasses understanding. He's got this! And us!"

This is just part of the reason she is my friend. She didn't take any time to feel sorry for herself or worry about the unknown; she trusted. She'd been asked to walk out her faith in a real, tangible way, so she started walking. While I was busy driving around San Antonio and crying every time I heard Christy Nockels sing "Healing Is in Your Hands," Jen was praising him for peace and the provision he knew she'd need before she ever even needed it.

As time went by and the plan to treat Jen's cancer became clearer, Gulley and I began to figure out a time to go to Dallas to help out for a few days. Our original plan was to drive to Dallas, but since gas was about $74 a gallon that summer, it made more sense to fly after we realized Southwest was running some kind of special fare. So I booked our flights and we counted down the days, because when one of your best friends is sick, you just want to get there and see her in person and know that she's okay.

I'd never thought about it much before that trip, but in all the years Gulley and I have been friends, we hadn't flown many places together. And traveling by air is a different animal than taking a road trip. Normally when I fly I like to bring a book or a bunch of magazines, but I knew Gulley well enough to know that she was going to ask me why we were even flying somewhere together if all I was going to do was read a book, so I didn't even bother to pack one.

Over the last few years, I've flown quite a bit, so I've kind of gotten it down to a science. At least as much of a science as you can get when dealing with finicky airplanes and overzealous security and four-ounce containers of liquid. At some point, I'd apparently also voiced my objection to having to check our bags instead of carrying them on, because Gulley kept apologizing to me for not having a bag that was small enough to carry on.

I finally asked, "Why are you so worried about it?"

And she replied, "Because you hate traveling with people that check bags. You told me that."

I had no recollection of this, but I know it's true, because I tend to go off on passionate rants about things that I really don't feel that strongly about in the grand scheme of life. And I guess at some point checked luggage fell into that category. Other favorite rant subjects include Chinese food, pizza with thick crust, the way library books smell, and motorized carts at the grocery store.

So after many assurances to Gulley that she could check her bag and that her purse didn't really count as a carry-on item, we finally made it to the airport the morning of our flight. And it turned out that all the discussion was for naught, because her bag was small enough to carry on even though she worried it didn't fit in the Southwest carry-on "sample" bin. I've always believed that the sample bin is just a suggestion, not a rule. How else do you explain some of the monstrosities they allow people to put in the overhead compartments?

We wheeled our bags through the security line, but then Gulley's bag got flagged for a hand check. They had to confiscate her bottle of Big Sexy Hair Spray. This meant two things. First, Gulley was going to have flat, unsexy hair in Dallas, which was a shame, because you really need your biggest, sexiest hair when taking care of your friend who has cancer. Second, she apologized to me again for being a high-maintenance traveler.

(Related note: You would think that security wouldn't be concerned about a bottle of Big Sexy Hair flying between two Texas cities. It seems like a given.)

As we walked to the gate, I assured her it was fine. That kind of stuff happens. But then she confessed that she didn't want to be a pain to travel with, because she really wanted to go with me on my book tour. And this is why I love her. She believed in me enough to think there was going to be a book tour. Where I'd fly to places. In reality, the closest thing I had to a book tour was driving to the neighborhood Walmart and putting up a poster board that read "BOOK SIGNING."

We made it to Dallas, and the rest of the afternoon was spent catching up with Jen while Linc took a nap and then walking to the park, where we met some more of Jen's friends. And Gulley and I were reminded of how hard it is to have a group of toddlers— especially toddlers who thought they were going to get to swim only to discover that the pool was closed and their only option was hot playground equipment. Sad times. But Linc got to crawl around and eat some playground mulch, so the adventure wasn't a total bust.

Later on that evening, Gulley and I made a run to the store to stock up on essential snack items for a girls' night so we could all settle in and spend the night catching up on everything that was going on. This is a short way to tell you we bought a lot of products that contained cheese and chocolate. We'd recently learned that Jen's cancer had spread to her lymph nodes, and we wanted the real story on what she was facing, not just the happy, smiley, "Let's kick cancer's butt" e-mail version.

By this time, Jen had already gone through enough chemo treatments that she'd begun to lose her hair, and a sweet woman who'd had cancer several years before gave Jen her wigs. The original wig was named Pinky. Then she gave Jen a second wig that wasn't quite as nice, and we just referred to it as Pinky's cheap sister. She told Jen she could cut them or do whatever she wanted with them, and Jen's goal was to have one cut into a simple bob and the other one long enough to pull into a ponytail or a messy bun. It's always good to have hair options, especially when you have no hair of your own.

While we were visiting, a friend of Jen's stopped by to see what kind of magic she could work with Pinky and her cheap sister. She explained that she wasn't a licensed hair stylist, but she'd been cutting hair forever and also styled hair for weddings and special events, and she was excited to help Jen. As we talked, I couldn't quit looking at her bangs. They were very similar to the bangs of my dreams. I felt like they were the bangs I'd been looking for all my life. Bangs that looked like Reese Witherspoon's. I asked her if she thought she could cut my bangs to look like hers, and she said she could. It was like a dream come true.

That's how I ended up having my hair cut and styled by an unlicensed beautician while I was supposedly in town to nurse my sick friend back to health. And it's also the reason why bobby pins were my best friend for the next six months after this bad hair decision. The truest thing I've ever heard is that every woman who cuts her bangs immediately begins the process of growing them back out again.

But back to that night. Jen was facing her hardest round of chemo the next morning, and I guess that's why none of us really wanted to quit talking and attempt to go to sleep. True to form, the later it got, the punchier we all got, until we decided that what we really wanted to do was toilet-paper someone's house.

(I would refer to this as wrapping a house. Some people say rolling a house. Maybe it's regional? Or generational? I don't know.)

Anyway, I can't really explain why we were so enamored with the idea other than it's perfectly normal for a bunch of forty-year-old women to load up a twelve-pack of Charmin and hit the neighborhood. Initially we were going to wrap our friend Hite's place, but we ultimately decided on Jamie's house, because she has three boys and we figured she would never suspect us, because who wraps houses at our age?

Apparently we do.

So we woke Jen's husband to let him know we'd be back in a little while after we finished wrapping a house, and to his credit he didn't even question us or our sanity. Then we loaded up in the car, piled the toilet paper in the baby's car seat, and headed out like a group of twelve-year-old girls. Except without all the fake drama and high-pitched squeals and Taylor Swift sing-alongs. Okay, so maybe there was a Taylor Swift sing-along. Whatever.

As we circled the block calculating our plan of attack, Gulley voiced a concern that the police might show up and arrest us. But we decided we could just explain that Jen couldn't spend the night in jail since she had a chemo treatment early the next morning and a baby waiting for her at home.

I'm sure they hear that all the time.

We opted for comfort over stealth and parked right in front of Jamie and Trevor's house and went to work. Sadly, it became evident that our toilet-papering skills weren't what they used to be. I must have thrown one roll of Charmin in the air fifty times before I could get it over a tree limb, but ultimately our decidedly un-ninja-like skills paid off, and we made a clean getaway. Then we went home and crashed.

The next morning Gulley and I kept Linc while Jen went to chemo, and we realized we'd forgotten how exhausting it is to have a one-year-old. I'm sad to report that it took both of us to change his diaper, even though I tried to be a self-righteous diaper changer and told Gulley, "Here, just let me do it" right before he squirmed out of my reach and crawled his naked bottom away from us as fast as he could. This was after a morning of going on a walk and blowing bubbles and rolling a ball back and forth and petting the dog multiple times, and as we sat exhausted on the front porch, Gulley looked at me and announced, "It's only 9:15."

Jen made it home from chemo, took a nap, and felt fine the rest of the night. We were able to catch up some more and eat dinner and just enjoy being together. But we refrained from wrapping any more houses.

That night as we crawled into bed, I told Gulley that our visit to Dallas caused my inner junior high girl to come out. Maybe it was the reaction to seeing my friend so sick, or maybe I just needed to blow off steam, but in the span of twenty-four hours I had let someone I barely know cut my hair just because I thought hers looked cute and threw a twelve-pack of perfectly good toilet paper all over a friend's yard. All that was lacking was to call someone and then hang up when they answered and to unlock my diary to write all about the heartache of seventh grade while listening to Air Supply, and the cycle would have been complete.

But beyond haircuts or chemo or toilet paper, our time in

Dallas was precious to me. It's that indescribable quality of old friends. You can tell new friends about a story from your past, and they may laugh and appreciate it, but the old friends lived it with you. They remember the 1965 Mustang you all had to push across Villa Maria the night it died or that you've never been a fan of someone asking how you REALLY are or those ugly red jeans from Express that you never should have worn. You can tell them a story without having to fill in all the details, because they know the details already. They can look across the table at you and say, "That situation hasn't changed in twenty-three years" and make you feel normal because you know they get it. They get you. They're your safe place when you need just a few hours of normal in between the hard times in life, and they're your coconspirators when you get the urge to wrap someone's house.

A couple of months later, Jen was finished with surgery and chemo. She called Gulley and me to see if we might be interested in meeting her in College Station for the weekend. Her husband was leaving to go on a fishing trip, so it was a great time for her to get out of town with the baby, because everyone knows it's no fun being home alone with a fifteen-month-old when you can just drive a few hours and be with people who will spoil him rotten and possibly let you sleep in.

It turned out that Gulley and her family were already planning on making the trip since they had tickets to the football game. And it doesn't really take more than whispering the words, "Do you want to go to Bryan?" for me to start packing a suitcase, no questions asked.

So on Friday afternoon, Caroline and I hopped in the car with

Gulley, Jon, and their boys to make the trip. After three hours in the car (Three hours that I had to mind-over-matter my car sickness, because I don't do well in the backseat. Or the front seat. Or really any seat that isn't me driving.), we finally arrived at Honey and Big's house, and Jen and Lincoln were already there. It had been a rough month of surgery and doctors' reports for Jen, and Gulley and I were both so happy to hug her in person and cover Linc in the kind of kisses he'll dread getting from us as he gets older.

Not only that, but Nena decided to bust out of her assisted living home for the evening and join in the festivities. We sat around the kitchen table and caught up. Jen told Nena the story of how she and Scott got engaged after more than a year of being broken up, and I knew by the light in Nena's eyes that there wasn't a person in her universe who wouldn't know that story by Saturday afternoon.

Gulley, Jen, and I stayed up visiting for so long that we might as well have gone to Midnight Yell Practice, even though we'd decided earlier that we were too tired. But midnight came and went. And then one o'clock came and went. Finally, just shy of two o'clock in the morning, we decided we'd better pack it in so we wouldn't be too tired for the game-day festivities.

Saturday morning dawned with kolaches and chocolate donuts from Shipley's. Linc woke up bright and early the way babies tend to do. But Honey got him out of bed, and by the time Jen woke up, Linc was already enjoying his first chocolate donut. And clearly he's a genius, because it took him three seconds to realize it was far superior to the grapes he'd been eating earlier.

After we lounged around for an appropriate amount of time, we got dressed and headed to campus for all the pregame activities. Gulley's husband, Jon, had taken the boys out earlier to see Lee Corso and the ESPN crew, but Caroline decided to hang with the girls and appointed herself chief caretaker of Linc. It's not often that she gets to be the boss of someone, and she took her role very seriously.

When the game was over, we picked up barbecue for dinner, and then Tiff stopped by to hang out. Life had gotten so busy for all of us that it had been several years since we'd all been together. Which was why Gulley insisted we take a picture even though we were all sans makeup and in our pajamas. After checking the pictures on my phone, I complained that my bangs looked terrible in the first one, and Gulley didn't like her hair all pulled back, and then Jen trumped us both by reminding us that she's bald. And then we laughed until we cried, because in what surreal universe does one of us have cancer?

More than twenty years ago, the four of us spent countless hours at Honey and Big's house. We baked cookies, did laundry, ate meals, pretended to study, tried out new hairstyles, and laid the foundation for friendships that have withstood the tests of time and distance. And that Saturday night, we sat huddled on the couch together in a little cocoon of happiness and maybe a little bit of denial that so many years had gone by so quickly. We were there together, enjoying every minute we had, until it was time for Tiff to pick up her teenage daughter from a party, which brought us to the astonishing realization that we're old enough to have teenagers.

The whole thing was just a gift. An indescribable gift. The blessing of friends who continue to inspire me year after year.

The next morning Jen left early because she had to get back to Dallas before driving to Houston early Monday morning to go to MD Anderson. We hugged good-bye and kissed the baby and told Jen to keep us updated on everything. And then we cried as she drove away, because the weekend was over too soon and we just wanted her to be better and she was so brave—even though she'll read this and text me to tell me she wasn't that brave and she just did what the doctors told her to do.

(Side note: At one point during all this, Jen told us that people kept telling her they were praying for her recovery, and she said what she really needed were prayers to be a better wife and mother, so she just told Jesus to redirect the prayers that way. Please don't miss that she told Jesus what to do. I love her so much.)

Eventually, Gulley and I got all our stuff packed up and the kids loaded in the car so we could make the drive back to San Antonio. She and I sat in the backseat while Jon drove and Jackson sat in the front seat beside him. Jackson had the iPod and decided he was our DJ for the trip. And as we headed out, he put on Chris Tomlin singing "How Great Is Our God." Gulley and I looked at each other as we felt the tears come, and she grabbed my hand and held it as we listened:

> *How great is our God—sing with me . . .*
> *Name above all names*
> *Worthy of all praise*
> *My heart will sing*
> *How great is our God*

At that moment we were both overwhelmed with gratitude for a weekend full of priceless memories and the realization that God had given us a miracle in Jen. She still had a ways to go, but she was going to make it to the other side of this. God had spared us from a bridge none of us was ready to cross.

We live in a world where tomorrows are never guaranteed and pain lurks around every corner. Sometimes you just have to take a deep breath and acknowledge that you've been given a gift—that you've been in the presence of a living, breathing miracle.

And then Jackson put on "Thunderstruck" by AC/DC. Which was, needless to say, incredibly soothing and also our entrance back into reality.

As I was working on the final edits for this book, we found out that Jen's cancer has returned. Barring a miracle, her doctors have told her she most likely has about two years left. Two years. Obviously this isn't the way I wanted this story to go, and like Jen said on the phone the other day, it makes me think an alternate title for this book could be *Nobody's Sadder than Me*.

The thing is that even in the midst of this tragic news, we still find ourselves laughing through our tears. Jen told me that her husband, Scott, has been amazed at the outpouring of love and support for her. He said he was such an introvert before he married her that he could have been dead for weeks before anyone would have noticed. But it's such a testament to who Jen is that we are falling all over ourselves to do anything we can to make this road easier for her.

When she told us the sad news, she referenced the story of Shadrach, Meshach, and Abednego from Daniel 3, where they faced the fiery furnace and declared (I'm paraphrasing), "Our God is able to deliver us, but even if he doesn't, we will serve him anyway."

Sometimes the things that make sense in light of eternity don't make sense while we're still walking it out here on earth. Yet we will trust him; yet we will praise him.

And just in case Kathie Lee Gifford is reading this, one of Jen's bucket-list items is to be on the *Today* show with me. Can we please make that happen? No pressure.

CHAPTER 19

The Wonder of It All

So much of me
Is made of what I learned from you
You'll be with me
Like a handprint on my heart
STEPHEN SCHWARTZ

ON A FRIDAY morning several weeks ago, just after I'd gotten home from dropping Caroline off at school and was feeding the puppies breakfast, I pulled my phone out of my purse and noticed I'd a missed call from Gulley. She calls me every morning on her way to work, but it's usually about 8:20 when she calls, and today it was just a little after 8:00. (You'd be amazed at how many problems we can solve in ten minutes as she drives to the preschool where she teaches.)

I called her back, figuring she'd left early to pick up donuts for work or something, but I knew something was wrong as soon as she answered the phone. I don't even think she said hello. There was just a sob, and I asked, "What's wrong?"

She said, "We've lost Nena."

This shouldn't have felt like a punch in the gut. No one would say it's a shock to lose a ninety-year-old woman with a bad heart, but we felt shocked nonetheless. She caught us all by surprise.

Two and a half years earlier, Gulley's granddaddy had passed away, and Nena had had a heart attack two weeks later. The doctors warned the family that her heart was in bad shape and said she probably had anywhere from two weeks to two months to live. But then she made it past those two months. And then a year. And then two years. I guess we just all began to believe that those doctors had no idea what they were talking about.

Not to mention that she never stopped being fully Nena. She always wanted to hear all about what the kids were doing and what color lipstick Gulley was wearing and where I'd bought whatever purse I happened to be carrying. She'd tell us stories that she heard on the news, like the one about a woman who had survived at sea wearing only a bikini top on her head to protect her from the sun for nineteen days. Then Nena would laugh and say, "Or maybe it was only nineteen hours! I can't remember!"

She'd fill us in on the news in her assisted living home and wave her hands as she dismissed "the old people who do those puzzles all the time." Honey asked her one afternoon if she wanted to go downstairs and hear a guest musician play the bagpipes, and she replied, "Why on earth would I want to go listen to some old man play the bagpipes?"

The Sunday before she died, her youngest son had come to visit, and she asked, "Where did you get your hair cut?"

And when he told her, she said, "Well, don't ever go there again. It looks terrible."

I loved her so much.

We all did.

Because the thing about Nena was that she never failed to make you feel better after you'd spent time with her. She had an easy laugh and a quick smile, and she was the best listener. One of Honey's friends called her on Sunday morning and made the comment that it's hard to lose someone who was your biggest fan. And that's how Nena was. She made us all feel like she was our biggest fan.

Anyway, it took me a minute to process what Gulley was telling me, and then I felt my own tears well up as my grief over the loss and my sadness for Gulley came to the surface. We hung up pretty quickly because she wanted to call and check on her mom and because Jon was waiting for her, but I told her to call me back as soon as she knew more. And then I sat in a chair on my back porch and began to cry.

After a few minutes I got up and began to do the only thing I knew to do, because I had that feeling of being helpless but wanting to do something productive. Isn't that what so often happens to us when someone we love is hurting? I gathered up my best black dresses, a pair of black pumps, a few different necklaces, and some earrings and then got into the car to drive to Gulley's house. Some people bring food in times of grief, but apparently I bring clothing and accessories. I just knew she would want to get to Bryan to be with her family as soon as possible, and packing a suitcase with things she actually needs has never been Gulley's strong suit, even when she's not grieving a loss.

Jon opened the door for me when I got to the house, because my hands were full with dresses and bags of accessories. Gulley rounded the corner from her bedroom to the living room, and we just fell in each other's arms and started to cry as Jon quietly took the dresses out of my hands and retreated to the bedroom.

We sat down on the couch while she filled me in on what she'd heard from her mom. Nena didn't wake up when they went in that morning to check on her, but the night before she'd spent an hour on the phone with her best friend, Jo, lamenting that the hairdresser she'd gone to that day had made her look like an old lady and she'd had to comb the whole thing out and put her own rollers in her hair to try to fix it. She passed away later that night, sleeping peacefully in her bed with Velcro rollers in her hair. And I think that's the part that really got to Gulley and me—that Nena had spent the last night of her life on the phone with her best friend.

Nena and Jo had lived down the street from each other since they were young women. They worked on their marriages, raised their babies, shared life and gossip, and shopped at more than their share of garage sales together. For decades, not a day went by when they didn't talk on the phone or pop in to see each other. One of my very favorite stories is one they told about a time when someone in their Sunday school class passed away. Jo decided to make some soup to take over to the family's home, so Nena decided to make some sweet cornbread muffins to accompany the soup.

Nena baked her muffins and wrapped them up for the family but saved two of them for her and Granddaddy to eat with their lunch later on. She and Jo delivered the meal, and then Nena came home, fixed lunch, and took a bite of her cornbread muffin. She said it was the worst-tasting thing she'd ever put in her mouth and spit it out. It was so bad she couldn't even swallow it. She ran to the kitchen to try to figure out what had gone wrong. And that's when she saw the potential problem. Instead of spraying the muffin tins with Pam cooking spray, she suspected she'd sprayed them with a can of OFF! mosquito repellent.

She called Jo and told her she needed her to come down to

the house immediately, and as Jo walked through the door, Nena said, "Jo! I think I may have just poisoned our Sunday school class! Taste one of these muffins and see if you think I sprayed the pan with OFF!"

Because why wouldn't you ask your best friend to verify whether you'd just poisoned your Sunday school friends by having her taste to make sure?

As we talked about how perfect it was that Nena and Jo had spent an hour on the phone the night before Nena died, Gulley said to me, "That's the thing about Nena—she knew how to be a great friend. She was my first friend, and she taught me how to be a friend."

What a legacy to leave. The legacy of friendship.

I learned about friendship from my grandmothers as well. I used to spend the night with Me-Ma when I was a little girl, and I always knew I'd wake up in the morning and find her sister, Mamie, sitting at the breakfast table with her, drinking coffee and discussing whatever or whoever needed discussing that day. I can still hear the sound of their laughter and remember how Me-Ma would get so tickled she'd have to wipe her tears with her apron. Later in the day she'd pick up that old rotary-dial phone in the kitchen so they could talk again.

And my grandmother Nanny never failed to make friends wherever she went. People were drawn to her and her ability to make everything more fun.

These women showed me how to love and how to laugh and what it looks like to invest in the people around you. I still think of both of them so often and miss them so much. There is something about the women of that generation—they really knew what it meant to raise your family and make your home and your friends your true ministry. Their girl friends were the very beat of their hearts.

Someone once said to Gulley, "To have a Mel, you have to be a Gulley."

To which Gulley replied, "To have a Gulley, you have to be a Mel."

We both learned how to be a friend by watching the women who came before us. Women who taught us that it's okay to show someone who you really are—that when you stop hiding behind a mask of perfection and protection, you unlock something beautiful. We can say, "I'm hurting," "My marriage is struggling," "My kid is failing math," "I don't want to get out of bed in the morning," "My pants are too tight," or "I don't see God in any of this" and know that the other person will not only help us find the part of ourselves we've lost but also see us safely to the shore. Our girl friends weave a luminous thread from the women we are to the women we hope to become. We may never find perfection, but we'll never be alone.

As I watch Caroline navigate friendships in junior high, I realize how important it is for her to have an example of what real friendship is and that it looks a lot like 1 Corinthians 13:

Love never gives up.
Love cares more for others than for self.
Love doesn't want what it doesn't have.
Love doesn't strut,
Doesn't have a swelled head,
Doesn't force itself on others,

Isn't always "me first,"
Doesn't fly off the handle,
Doesn't keep score of the sins of others,
Doesn't revel when others grovel,
Takes pleasure in the flowering of truth,
Puts up with anything,
Trusts God always,
Always looks for the best,
Never looks back,
But keeps going to the end.

I CORINTHIANS 13:4-7, *The Message*

A good friend will love you, support you, and cheer you on. A good friend doesn't make you feel inadequate or like you're not good enough. A good friend won't dump you when someone better comes along or ask you to compromise who you are and what you believe.

These are the lessons we need to instill in the young women who are coming behind us, because there are few things in life worth having as much as a few close friends, and it's worth trading popularity for authenticity. In this new world we've built of Facebook friends and Instagram likes and texting instead of listening to an actual voice, it's still worth going deeper and finding people who will love you for your real, authentic, broken self. And, most important: to find that person means we have to be that person.

The weekend after Nena passed away, Gulley was at her mom's house, and her mom's friend Cindy had come to visit. Cindy told them they needed to lie down and get some rest because they had a long few days ahead of them, and they agreed. Then, as Cindy was leaving, Nena's best friends, Jo and Dorothy Kay, pulled up to the house. Cindy walked over to them and said, "They're going to rest right now. You should probably come back later."

As Cindy began walking to her car, Jo looked at Dorothy Kay and asked, "What do you think we should do?"

Dorothy Kay replied, "Wait until she drives off and then go inside."

Because they wanted to be with the people who belonged to their best friend, and nothing was going to stop them. That's the legacy of friendship.

(Cindy laughed later, saying she totally knew that's what they were planning to do, and Gulley and I said that in all fairness, if someday one of our kids tried to take charge of this type of situation, we wouldn't listen to them either.)

Which brings me back to the friendship between Jonathan and David. When David heard of Jonathan's death on the battlefield, he wept and declared, "Your friendship was a miracle-wonder, love far exceeding anything I've known—or ever hope to know" (2 Samuel 1:26, *The Message*).

And that's ultimately what God has given us in the people he has placed in our lives as he knits our souls with theirs: a miracle. A grace-filled, life-changing, soul-refreshing miracle.

May we never lose the wonder of it all.

The World according to Gulley and Mel

OVER THE COURSE of our friendship, Gulley and I have developed a bit of our own language—words and phrases that allow us to completely understand what the other one is trying to say without any further explanation. Feel free to adopt any of these as your own. Or maybe you'd like to get them embroidered on a nice throw pillow or painted artfully on a canvas. Either way.

1. It's a good day for chicken in the bed.

   This is what we say when it's a rainy day or when we're both tired and wish we could just hang out together and do nothing.

2. I don't believe I'd-a told that.

   Gulley's dad introduced us to this phrase many years ago when someone he worked with told him a story that was way too personal. We now use it on a regular basis when someone shares a little more than you needed to know.

3. Well.

Yep. That's it. Just a simple "Well." Depending on the tone and style in which it's uttered, it can mean anything from "Nobody cares about that" to "I'm going to need some time to think about this."

For example, when our kids come in from outside and are trying to tell on each other for something stupid, like who kicked the football across the yard, either Gulley or I will say, "Well . . . ," which essentially means, "Go figure it out, because we aren't wasting words on this dumb bit of minutia." And the kids know that this is what we're saying, because they'll get mad and reply, "I can't believe all you said was 'Well.'" To which we usually respond, "And we can't believe you dumb-dumbs are fighting over who's going to walk five feet to pick up the football."

4. Kinfolk, you did that.

One of my high school friends wrote this on Facebook after his cousin did something embarrassing, and I thought it was the funniest thing I'd ever heard. Now Gulley and I use it when one of us does something stupid.

5. If you marry a fool, then you slowly become a fool.

Not a saying so much as a cautionary piece of advice straight from Gulley's mouth.

6. Nobody's sad when your dog dies except you.

This is something Gulley said years ago, and I've found it to be true. People may tell you they're sorry your dog died and truly mean it, but they aren't actually grieving for your dog.

7. My friend!

We start basically every phone conversation this way. It's our standard greeting as opposed to the more boring "Hello."

8. Let me tell you what your friend did. . . .

When we're annoyed at someone, usually a spouse or one of our children, we refer to that person as the other's friend. For example: "Let me tell you what your friend Caroline did this morning on the way to school."

9. Just a splash . . .

If we really want a glass of wine but are trying to be good, we opt to call it "just a splash."

10. Get a hold of yourself.

Occasionally one of us (usually me) tends to get a little worked up over something that may not warrant a level-ten reaction for a level-two situation. This is our way of saying, "Simmer down."

11. Don't go eating in other people's deep freeze. You don't know what people do in their deep freeze.

This piece of advice was given to Gulley by a coworker many years ago. It has stuck with us, and you'd be amazed how many times it's proven to be beneficial. The truth is, you don't know what people do in their deep freeze.

12. If you'll lie, you'll cheat; if you'll cheat, you'll steal; if you'll steal, you'll steal from me.

Yet another piece of advice Gulley learned from a coworker. It's the truth. And you can feel free to move the verbs around to make it better apply to your individual situation.

13. Get excited, Coach Fran!

Gulley enjoys a good reaction and occasionally gets annoyed if I don't seem excited enough about something. This is a reference to former Aggie football coach Dennis Franchione, who never showed an ounce of emotion on the sidelines, no matter what was happening during the game. It frustrated us to no end.

14. You are the bigger person.

We've always maintained that sometimes the worst part of acting in a benevolent way toward someone who may not deserve it is that no one tells you that you're the bigger person. We make it a policy to let the other know that she is the bigger person in any situation that calls for it.

15. I'll tell you one thing . . .

There is never just one thing. This is just a segue into a litany of thoughts and opinions. We just like to start things out with an emphatic statement.

16. Okay.

Honestly, we didn't realize this was one of our words until my friend Angie came to visit and we all went out to eat together. At the end of the night she remarked that she'd never known people who could use the word *okay* to convey so many different reactions, whether it be concern, excitement, or empathy.

Here are two different "okay" scenarios:

Mel: I just found out that our contractor can't finish our bathroom for two more weeks, and I'm so frustrated.

Gulley: Okaaaayyy.

Or:

Gulley: Jon's going out of town this weekend. Want to get together with the kids on Friday night?

Mel: OKAY!!!!!

17. Nobody's cuter than you.

Hence the title of this book. This is what we tell each other when one of us is having a bad day or just found another wrinkle by her eyes or realized all that toffee she ate over the Christmas holidays did, in fact, show up on her hips.

Thirty-Seven Reasons to Love Mel

By Gulley

NOTE FROM MEL: I realize it probably seems a little gratuitous to include a list of reasons why someone loves you in a book you've written. But I felt like this was an opportunity for you to see things from Gulley's point of view. You have to understand that this list is a big deal, because Gulley maintains she would never be a writer since all she would ever write is "Today I did laundry. I drove the car pool. I cooked chicken for dinner and served rice as a side dish. Then I went to bed."

Personally, I don't think she gives herself enough credit, because that's compelling stuff.

Anyway, the following is by Gulley. You will notice that there are thirty-seven things listed because she originally wrote this on my thirty-seventh birthday. Let's hope she could add six more things to this list now that I'm forty-three.

1. We laugh hysterically every day.
2. If we skip a day, we make up for it by laughing double the next day.

3. She randomly hates things. For example: "I hate pizza." "I hate Chinese food."

4. She will hate things on my behalf. For example: "I hate [insert store name here] for being rude to you."

5. She has given me fashion advice for many years.

6. She finds clothes and accessories for me, even if they would not suit her.

7. We have an unspoken hierarchy of the type of therapy needed for certain problems: cookie dough by the spoonful, queso, or a margarita.

8. The girl can cook.

9. When she cooks something I like, she will call and say, "Come over. I made _____."

10. We have shown up to drop the kids off at school wearing the same thing more than once.

11. She's not easily offended, and all the sensitive people want to be her friend.

12. Many times one of us has picked up the phone to call the other while the other was dialing.

13. She makes everything more fun.

14. She rarely complains about anything.

15. She is very tender and will cry with me when I cry.

16. She gives sound advice.

17. She loves God and his Word.

18. On Thanksgiving we say the same thing every year: "Of all the things I have to be thankful for, you are in my top five!"

19. She will go Christmas shopping with me all over town even when she is done with her shopping.

20. On any given day, our conversation pendulum will swing from questions like, "Is my faith thrilling and delightful?"

to "What color velour is best?" and "What are the top fashion finds right now?"

21. She DID buy our entire Bible study group blue-suede fringe bracelets to wear during *Believing God.* She did NOT spend more time deliberating on the fringe than on the actual Bible study.

22. She always knows what to say and what not to say. Even if it means telling me my husband is right.

23. She will run something over for you to wear on a moment's notice.

24. She will pore over photos and magazines with you to find the perfect hairstyle.

25. She will listen and listen and listen and listen.

26. She is witty.

27. She loves my boys and bonds with them by playing UNO and games on the Wii and going to T-ball games.

28. We share a passion for Aggie sports, especially football.

29. We both complete NCAA basketball brackets.

30. The person you see on the blog—she is all that and more. Oh yes ma'am, she is!

31. We can talk baseball better than two guys ever could.

32. I believe we will all have hair like hers when we get to heaven. She has no self-righteousness about this.

33. We include each other in our big moments.

34. When I start trash-talking at sporting events, she is polite at first but eventually joins in.

35. The first time we saw each other after we were both married, we stayed up talking about marriage until five o'clock in the morning. Then we wished aloud that stores opened at five o'clock so we could go shopping.

36. When we went to New York together, I literally spent my last dollar on a must-have tracksuit. She paid for my cab fare to the airport and my headphones on the flight home.

37. Because big news isn't big until I have shared it with her.

So You Want to Take a Road Trip

ONE OF THE questions I get asked most often is about the road trips Gulley and I take each summer with the kids. Some of them are regarding our basic sanity, but I won't get into specifics on that one, because I think the fact that we load up the car with our kids each summer speaks for itself. Clearly, we are not quite right in the head.

But several people have also wanted to know various specifics about how we do it. I can only assume this is because they are pondering this type of trip for themselves and someone they don't mind spending a week with under sometimes stressful conditions where kids think it's a good idea to wrestle on a hotel bed and knock over their mother's glass of wine after a long day of summertime fun.

The first thing you need to know is this: you always have to stop at Dairy Queen.

But there is so much more to our road trips than just the occasional DQ Blizzard. I hereby give you my nondefinitive guide to a summer road trip.

1. Find a friend who is willing to do this with you.

Preferably someone with a high tolerance for shenanigans, who won't judge you if at some point during the trip you threaten to drop all the children off at a fire station to see if they can be placed for adoption.

Also, you might want to find someone who doesn't have too many kids (unless you have access to a van or a bus rental). This is crucial because there is only so much room in the car for the children and the stuff.

I may be willing to hit the road for a week and test the limits of my patience, but I'm not doing it without my favorite pillows.

2. Choose the best vehicle for your travels.

Gulley and I have historically taken her car on road trips because it's bigger. Plus, her younger son, Will, is the most likely to throw up, and it's always more comforting to have a child throw up in the car you've paid for than in your friend's car.

However, there was a time that Will threw up in my car, and Gulley showed up at my house the next day with a gift card for a complete detailed car wash even after she'd scoured it from top to bottom looking for signs of throw-up. That's the sign of a good friend.

3. Pack plastic bags, wet wipes, and paper towels.

Road trips present many opportunities for car sickness and/or food poisoning. One of our lowest road-trip moments was the summer of 2010 when Will caught a stomach bug at the Great Wolf Lodge in Dallas, and we had to make the three-hour drive to Gulley's mom's house in Bryan while he threw up at fifteen-minute intervals into a plastic sack. This was the trip when we learned that you can never have too many plastic grocery sacks.

It was also the trip when we learned we could still eat beef jerky and sing along to Taylor Swift even while someone was puking in the background.

That's a life skill that will take you far.

4. Have a loose plan.

This is crucial. The first year we took the kids on a trip, we just went to Bryan to visit Gulley's family. We enjoyed it so much that we officially decided to make it an annual tradition. The road trip is ultimately our way of bringing a little old-school Americana into our kids' lives: the open road, the car sickness, the license plate game, and the arguments over whose foot just touched whose in the backseat. We always want it to be more about the journey than the destination—kind of like life.

Here's our philosophy: we keep it simple. The road trip is never about exotic sightseeing, unless you count the snake farm in New Braunfels. In which case, ACES.

Every year, after the road trip is over, we immediately begin to discuss where we might want to go the next year. We include the kids in the discussion too, even though we have ultimate veto power, because as much as we appreciate their input, it's impossible to drive to Australia.

As of now, we've always kept our trips in the state of Texas. This works out, because Texas is a very large state, and there is plenty to see within its borders. Also, we happen to have a lot of friends and family scattered around, and this usually gives us a convenient (free) place to stay on occasion.

We have gone to Dallas, Austin, Houston, Waco, Bryan/College Station, and various locales in between. We've visited the Dallas Zoo, ridden public transportation as entertainment, tried to ensure a future of chiropractic treatments at Six Flags in Dallas, "enjoyed" the Children's Museum in Waco, bought eighty-four pounds of beef jerky at Bucee's, walked all over the Texas A&M campus, cheered at Bombers baseball games, touched stingrays at the Houston Aquarium, eaten giant snow cones at an Astros game, visited the Baylor Bear, recorded our very own "Call Me Maybe" video, seen the Longhorns football stadium (sacrilege!), gone swimming at the Flying L water park in Bandera, toured the Texas Capitol building, and seen the Texas State History Museum.

Along the way, we've stopped to see glass-bottom boats, Barton Springs, a gas station/dance hall owned by Willie Nelson, several bakeries that sell kolaches, too many Dairy Queens to count, 6,075 public restrooms, and 5,462 Quik Marts/7-Elevens/Stop-N-Gos. We've sung too loud, argued too much, passed some gas, thrown up on our neighbors, and laughed enough to make it all worthwhile.

It's all about taking our time and being flexible enough to pull over the car when someone says, "Hey! We're in Waco! Let's go see the Baylor Bear!" or "Mom! I need to go to the bathroom again!"

Bottom line: I do not recommend this type of road trip for those who may be type A personalities and insist on a tight, well-scheduled agenda. That's a recipe for a meltdown.

5. Never underestimate the power of a good playlist.

Sometimes, just when you think you've reached the end of your mental rope, your best friend and copilot will put on Bon Jovi's "Living on a Prayer," and you'll decide that life is worth living again.

We usually go around the car and let everyone take turns making song requests, but the moms always have the right to veto a song choice if the thought of listening to Little Big Town sing "Boondocks" one more time is going to cause a grown-up to assume the fetal position for the rest of the day. Same goes for Taylor Swift, specifically "You Belong with Me." However, if a mom would like to listen to some old-school Bobby Brown songs a few times in a row, then it's her prerogative.

6. Split costs and stay within a budget.

I'm sorry if this tip led you to believe we make any sort of spreadsheets or pie charts. See above about type A personalities. It just means that we do try to keep things fairly inexpensive. Last summer we finally caved and did Six Flags, and that's probably the most expensive thing we've ever done, but we felt like the kids were now old enough to appreciate it.

The year we went to Great Wolf Lodge, our friend Alissa had won some passes, so that was inexpensive, with the exception of the food that gave us food poisoning once we got there. Then we try to look for passes or coupons for other things we may want to do. The good news is that riding the elevator up and down in the hotel is free. As is trying on sunglasses at Target.

Speaking of hotels, we always have good luck with Priceline. You can search according to how nice you'd like your hotel to be and the price you're willing to pay. Some cities have more to choose from than others, but we've always found a decent deal. It also became apparent last summer that the five of us can no longer pile into one hotel room, because everyone just keeps getting bigger and more aware of concepts like modesty and personal space. But we did one room for a long time and just brought along a sleeping bag and requested a rollaway for our extra person.

As for other costs, Gulley and I do our best to split everything down the middle. Again, there is no exact formula. She pays for gas one time, and I pay for it the next time. One morning she buys breakfast and snacks, and the next day I buy lunch and Sonic drinks. We believe it all comes out fairly even in the end. I also try to keep in mind that any activity is more expensive for her because she has one more kid than I do.

7. Google is your friend.

After we determine the main cities we'll be visiting, we consult the Google to research possible interesting stops between home and our destination. That doesn't mean we'll actually stop at all of them, but it gives us an idea of what our options are.

This can be as exotic as a gas station that sells tacos or as routine as a McDonald's with a playground.

8. Brushing your hair is optional.

In all seriousness, we try to make the trip feel like a fun adventure. Even though we occasionally have to lay down the mom smack, our goal is to be fun and leave a lot of our normal rules at home. This means a lot of candy, ice cream as a meal, no set bedtime, late night swimming at the hotel pool, and optional grooming. However, taking showers and brushing teeth are still required.

9. We're lovers, not fighters.

Sadly, this isn't always a given for the kids. However, it stands to reason that time in the car plus tired plus hot plus lots of activity can equal ill tempers. In the case that there are grievances to be aired, we try to opt for the "Y'all need to work it out" method. Sometimes this works, and sometimes it leads to more tears and yelling. In which case we opt for the "Everyone is going to their separate corners" approach. This usually involves a thirty-minute break from one another until we can regain composure and/or not want to "kick someone as hard as I can." There was also a time when Gulley's boys pushed her to the edge and caused her to declare she was "on the verge of a nervous breakdown." At that point we sent her to her room to regroup and offered to let her go get a pedicure.

Desperate times.

But in the end, we always do our best to love our road

trip neighbor because, as Gulley and I continually remind the kids, the road trip will go on even if we have to leave someone with a bad attitude behind.

10. Have fun and make memories.

I'll be honest. We've hit some lows on our road trips. People have gotten on each other's nerves. Some have overreacted when their song didn't get chosen as the next one played. Sometimes kids have acted ungrateful after their moms have spent a day at a water park being pummeled by waves. It's real life, but in a car.

But we've achieved our goal over the last seven summers. We have memories that make us howl with laughter. We have pictures that make us smile. We have stories that would make some people want to recoil in horror and fear.

We have logged a lot of miles together, and we don't regret a single one. More than anything, the summer road trip is our reminder that sometimes the best things in life are the simple things.

And plastic bags from the grocery store.

Ten Characteristics of a Best Friend

HERE ARE SOME final thoughts for you to ponder about friendship—both in looking for a good friend and becoming one. Some of these may be more important than others. I'll let you decide for yourself.

1. She'll let you borrow her favorite dress, shoes, jacket, or top when you need something cute to wear. Bonus points if she actually says in the dressing room, "I'll buy this, and then we can both wear it!"
2. Your name is safe on her lips. She won't tell your secrets or say anything behind your back that she wouldn't say to your face.
3. She won't tell your embarrassing stories without your permission, and she is always laughing with you, not at you.
4. She'll wait at least six hours before gently telling you that the person you're mad at may be right.
5. When you ask, "Can you do me a huge favor?" she answers "YES" before she even knows the rest of the sentence.

6. She forgives you for your PMS moods and occasional general state of grouchiness.

7. She's there for you when it feels like the whole world has turned upside down and life will never be okay again.

8. Even though she loves Chinese food, she recognizes that you don't and therefore never suggests it as a restaurant option when the two of you are together.

9. It's understood that if you're on a trip together, you share a hotel room. How else are you going to stay up all night talking?

10. On any given day, she's your sister, therapist, confidante, mother, nurse, chauffeur, hair technician, clothing stylist, nutritionist, and self-help guru who proclaims that you are good enough, kind enough, and doggone it, people like you. Otherwise known as declaring, "Nobody's cuter than you!"

About the Author

MELANIE SHANKLE LIVES in San Antonio, Texas, with her husband, Perry, and daughter, Caroline. She graduated from Texas A&M in 1994 while possibly on scholastic probation. Melanie began writing her blog, *Big Mama*, in July 2006, and she's the *New York Times* bestselling author of *Sparkly Green Earrings* and *The Antelope in the Living Room*. She's also a regular contributor to *The Pioneer Woman* blog. In her spare time she likes to shop good sales, watch too much television, and laugh at things that are sometimes inappropriate.

FOR MORE FROM *Melanie,*

check out

SPARKLY
GREEN
EARRINGS

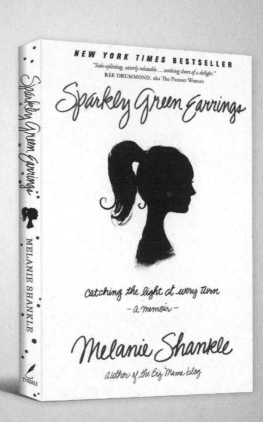

Sample the first chapter now.

CP0880

Death, Taxes, & Motherhood

I ALWAYS ASSUMED I'd have a child someday. Like death and taxes and Barbara Walters, it seemed like an inevitable part of life. But I can't remember the exact moment Perry and I decided it was time for us to bring our own little person into the world.

However, I can guarantee we didn't put nearly as much thought into it as we probably should have. I mean, it's a person we're talking about. We were making the decision to create and then raise a human being. Which is much different than a dog, despite all those well-meaning people who compare their experience of raising a puppy to having a baby.

And, by the way, I was that person. It makes me want to go back in time and gouge out my own eyes when I think of how many times I compared my best friend Gulley's stories of sleepless nights with her newborn son to my own harrowing tales of getting out of bed to let our puppy, Scout, outside to go to the bathroom.

Yes, that's the same.

Idiot.

I think Perry and I both had the same perception of parenthood—something along the lines of "How hard can this be? After all, we've raised a puppy." Which is probably the same thing Cujo's owner thought. And we all know how that turned out.

But if I really think hard (which is something I try not to do very often), I'd say the whole baby thing began as Perry and I drove home from a beach vacation one day in June 2001. We'd just spent three glorious days at the beach, fishing and reading and doing whatever other relaxing pastimes we used to do prior to becoming parents. I'd give you all the details, but this isn't that kind of book.

We had the windows down and the Beastie Boys turned up loud. (Don't judge. Beach vacations mean the Beastie Boys to me. It's who I am. A child of the eighties. You've got to fight for your right to party.) We were a couple of tanned, relaxed fools listening to bad rap music.

Then my cell phone rang. I turned down the music and flipped open my phone. Because this was back in the days of yore when phones still flipped open and were incapable of telling you how well you slept the night before or what you needed to buy at the grocery store or how many steps you took that day.

(I read somewhere about a guy whose wife whispered, "Mark of the beast, mark of the beast," every time he used his iPhone to get directions and it was able to pinpoint his exact location.)

(Don't think about that too long or it will freak you out.)

Anyway, I opened my phone, and Gulley greeted me with, "I'm pregnant!"

Immediately I felt tears sting my eyes. My heart did some kind of weird flip that on second thought may have actually been my arteries hardening up, courtesy of my steady vacation diet of various forms of processed snack foods.

I wasn't shocked to hear she was pregnant. After all, I'd been with her the week before and watched her devour an entire plate of triple-cheese enchiladas, which totally aroused my suspicions. That day she'd said it was too soon to know for sure if she was pregnant but admitted it was a possibility.

Three-cheese enchiladas plus a bowl of queso seemed to indicate there was a good chance a baby was looking for some calcium to build strong bones and some fat to build chubby, edible baby thighs.

I was right. She was pregnant, and I couldn't have been happier for her. But in my happiness there was this twinge of loneliness or sadness or some other emotion that I couldn't nail down. I mean, this was Gulley. My very best friend in the entire world. The person I'd shared a ten-by-ten room with all during college. The person who has loved me through all my ups and downs, who has seen me laugh the hardest and cry the most and encouraged me in everything from my faith in God to getting my bangs cut. The person who has known me since we believed there was no finer outfit in the world than a pair of plaid walking shorts with a denim shirt and some loafers. Worn with socks.

We've been together since the days we'd nail a beach towel over the window so we could nap all day before going out all night. College: it really is where idiots are born. Or at least where they thrive.

Now I was afraid she was moving on to exciting new things without me. We'd managed to get married within a month of each other. Probably because God knew we'd each need the other one to talk about all the things we didn't know about marriage, such as HUSBANDS EXPECT DINNER. But now she was headed toward full-on adulthood in the form of becoming someone's mother. She was moving on to things like wearing jeans that went all the way past her belly button and discussing the merits of different types of fruit snacks for school lunches.

(Considering that was my perception of motherhood, it should come as no surprise that it took me five years of marriage to even consider it.)

(Having a dog doesn't require any of those things.)

(Although Scout will eat a fruit snack, if the opportunity arises.)

I hung up my phone, looked at Perry, and announced, "Gulley's pregnant." He took his eyes off the road and glanced over at me, and I watched the color drain from his face. "You want one, don't you?" he said.

"I don't know. I haven't really thought about it. Maybe. I don't know," I answered. Which was all a total lie. The truth was I had thought about it. I'd thought about it a lot, and I knew I wanted a baby. Most likely a bunch of them. I may have even had a list of baby names prepared. I was ready to move on to the next phase in our lives.

My eyes must have conveyed my real answer because all of a

sudden he said, "I feel like I'm going to throw up. I may need to pull over and throw up."

What can I say? I married romance.

It's safe to assume that the last hour of our trip was much quieter than the previous stretch as we tried to ignore the enormous elephant that had just dropped between us onto the console of the car.

For the next few months we engaged in the occasional conversation about having babies and listed all the pros and cons—and then September 11 happened, and it seemed like a bad time to bring a baby into the world. Especially because Perry went into some kind of mode like he was a contestant on *Survivor* and we had to do things like stockpile bottled water and cans of Vienna sausages in our garage. Although, let's be honest—I would rather die in some apocalyptic event than eat meat that comes from a can.

And then came the day in January when I drove to Austin to be with Gulley while she delivered the most beautiful red-haired baby boy I'd ever seen. It didn't matter that her epidural didn't work the way it was supposed to or that I heard her actually growl when her husband had the poor judgment to enjoy a stick of beef jerky while she worked through a contraction. All that mattered was the barrel-chested, impossibly pink little boy in the nursery who made all the other babies seem sickly by comparison. All I could think was, *HOW CAN I GET ME ONE OF THOSE?*

But in spite of my fever for the babies, I knew we'd need to wait a little longer because we'd already committed to chaperone more than a hundred high school students on a spring break ski trip, and then we had plans to travel to Sicily with my parents so I could see the land of my ancestors. These are what you call first-world problems. Oh, we can't have a baby right now because we have to go to Colorado and ski and then go to Italy to tour Saint Peter's Basilica.

Looking back, I think the funniest part of all this is that we were under the illusion we were in control. That a baby would happen on our timetable, like we were a couple of fertile magicians pulling a rabbit out of a hat.

As it turned out, that wasn't exactly what God had planned for us. Yes, we would become parents (otherwise this would be a short book), but our path to getting there was harder and filled with more heartache than we'd counted on. I guess in a way it became our first lesson in the realities of parenthood. Which is to say, it can make you feel like a monkey in a windstorm.

Try these other titles from Tyndale House Publishers:

CP0738